GLUTEN-FREE

COOKING
FOR TWO

125 Favorites

CAROL FENSTER

Houghton Mifflin Harcourt
Boston • New York • 2017

For information about permission to reproduce selections from this book,
write to trade.permissions@hmhco.com or to Houghton Mifflin Harcourt
Publishing Company, 3 Park Avenue, 19th floor, New York, New York 10016.

www.hmhco.com

Library of Congress Cataloging-in-Publication Data is available.
ISBN 978-0-544-82868-1 (trade paper); 978-0-544-82873-5 (ebk)

Book design by Alison Wilkes

Printed in China
SCP 10 9 8 7 6 5 4 3 2 1

This book is lovingly dedicated
to my husband, Larry, and the
rest of my wonderful family.

Thanks for your love, support,
and encouragement while I
traveled this gluten-free journey
for the past three decades.

Contents

Introduction

A while back — in what I call a *BFO* (Blinding Flash of the Obvious) — I realized that I live in a two-person household, yet I've been cooking for the standard family-of-four household all my life. Of course, when I was writing all my previous cookbooks, I used the four-serving rule, but even when I wasn't in cookbook-writing mode, I still made large recipes. Think of all those leftovers and wasted food that spoiled before it was eaten — not to mention all of that space needed to store it!

And then, I looked around and realized my small household was like many others. How could I have missed this trend? It took phone calls and emails from my readers who asked for small-size recipes to bring me to the conclusion that the gluten-free world needs a comprehensive cookbook just for small households. So, I set about researching the small-household phenomenon.

Many People Live in Small Households

Today, more Americans are living in small households. Research shows that the traditional family-of-four image is irrelevant for many of us. Twenty-eight percent of the 115 million households in the U.S. were "solo" in 2011, compared with 26 percent in 2000. According to *USA Today,* the largest jump is among the seniors who are part of the 77 million baby boomers who became empty nesters when their kids left home. In this case, you once cooked for several people but now it's just the two of you. I can relate to this: My son (who ate so much while he was growing up that there were never any leftovers!) eventually grew up and left home, leaving my husband and me as the lone diners at our kitchen table.

In other cases, the small household isn't necessarily comprised of boom-

ers. In my travels around the country, I meet other "family" configurations: newly married couples, two-roommate households, one or two members within larger families who must eat differently than the rest of the family, and other nontraditional households.

You shouldn't have to give up your favorite foods just because you live in a small — rather than four-serving — household. You still deserve easy, healthy, delicious food that is tailored to your needs. I am always saddened to hear people say, "Oh, I don't cook much; after all, it's just me/the two of us. As though they no longer deserve to eat well since they aren't the "typical" family size! So, please get rid of the notion that your small household isn't important enough to justify cooking a meal. You, your health, and your happiness are the most important things.

I've tailored these recipes to serve two people because this is where there's the greatest need. However, if you're a single-person household, invite a friend or family member to join you, or pack the remaining portion for your lunch for tomorrow or freeze it for later in the week. Because paring down some recipes (especially baked goods) to one serving is simply not practical, I've formulated the recipes to yield at least two servings; even if you live alone, this shouldn't be an unmanageable size.

If you have celiac disease or gluten sensitivity, cooking for yourself and eating well is even more important because there is no pill or surgery to cure your health issues; eating gluten free is your only treatment. There's no reason to let "smallness" dampen your gluten-free culinary spirit.

So let's talk about what I call the cooking-for-two (or small-batch) kitchen. After all, small can be mighty!

The Cooking-for-Two Kitchen

Not only does small-batch cooking and baking make cute little parcels of food, it also gives you greater control over portion size and reduces your need for a lot of freezer or refrigerator space. It's just a more efficient way to live, as I've learned. I'm not always wondering how to use up that huge can of tomato juice, because I now buy juice in six-packs of 5.5-ounce cans, or that big jar of applesauce, because I buy individually packaged 4-ounce cups. (More on shopping for small-batch kitchens later.)

In addition, cooking small means less food waste because there are no leftovers that grow stale before you can finish them. Some experts have estimated American households throw away around 30 percent of their food; cooking food that is appropriately sized for your needs means less of it ends up in your wastebasket.

Now that you know the advantages, let's explore how to adapt your kitchen to a "cooking-for-two" style.

Appliances and Pans

Many of your existing appliances will still work when cooking for two, but there are some appliances that I believe are indispensable and that you should invest in to make this work for you. I mention brand names to let you know what I use, not to endorse the products.

BAKING PANS: Look for 5- or 6-inch nonstick (gray, not black) round baking pans. This size might be a bit hard to find; I use Wilton brand, which you may be able to find in specialty shops or online. A springform pan has a bottom that releases from the side and it is often used for cakes and cheesecakes. If you can find one, the cute 3-cup Bundt pan by Nordic Ware is perfect for small cakes. If you prefer to bake individual cakes, look for little 1-cup Bundt pans; their pretty shapes make especially elegant cakes.

BAKING SHEETS: You will need both nonstick (gray, not black) and regular (shiny) baking sheets, preferably 9x13 inches with rimmed edges. Use the nonstick sheets for roasting vegetables. The regular (shiny, not nonstick) sheets work well for certain kinds of cookies that don't require extensive browning on the bottom. Baking sheets can also be used for one-pan meals where you bake the starch, protein, and vegetables (in staggered times) on one sheet, like the Sheet Pan Supper of Roasted Fish and Vegetables on page 122.

Standard 9x13-inch baking sheets can also double as pizza pans, although a 12-inch round nonstick (gray, not black) pizza pan also works for making a small pizza.

BLENDER: I use a standard, 5-cup blender that is twenty years old. Except for replacing the glass jar occasionally, it still runs like the Energizer Bunny. It is perfect for blending batches of soup that a handheld blender would struggle to handle. (See Handheld Blender below.)

CONVENTIONAL OVEN: My oven is a double-wall conventional electric KitchenAid. It has a convection option, but I never use it because gluten-free baking does not work well in convection ovens. These ovens burn hotter, making gluten-free items bake faster, even though they prefer longer, slower baking periods to rise properly and cook through completely. In short, convection ovens often mean failed baked goods. For that reason, I don't use a convection oven in this book.

COOKTOP: I have a glass Electrolux cooktop, which has both electric and induction burners. The recipes in this book were tested on the electric burners only.

FOOD PROCESSOR: You can still use your standard-size food processor, but I also use my little mini-prep (3-cup) version (by Cuisinart or KitchenAid) for small jobs such as making bread crumbs from leftover or stale gluten-free bread.

HANDHELD (IMMERSION) BLENDER: An immersion blender is like a wand with sharp rotary blades on the end. It is perfect for blending small sauces and soups right in the pot rather than transferring to a blender or food processor. The whip attachment can be used instead of a portable mixer for mixing some batters. Look for models with blades that detach for easy cleaning in the dishwasher. My older model does not disassemble, so I immerse the blades in a pan of hot, soapy water, give it a buzz, and then dip it into hot water for a rinse before letting it dry in the dish rack.

LOAF PANS: These nonstick pans (gray, not black) are the workhorses in a small-batch kitchen. You will need the standard 4x8-inch and 5x9-inch pans for baking certain entrées such as lasagna — and also quick breads, brownies, and bars. For smaller loaf pans, look for pans that come close to measuring 3¼x5¾ inches. They may be listed as 3x5-inch or 4x6-inches; either size will work.

I prefer a loaf pan with lips on the ends so that I can easily grip it with an oven mitt when removing it from the oven. These brands include Wilton, available in specialty kitchenware stores and online, and Baker's Secret and Good Cook, which can be found in grocery stores. Unlike other brands, they are also seamless on the inside, making them easier to wash.

MICROWAVE OVEN: Mine is a no-frills model with 1,000 watts, but I use it every day for gently reheating leftovers; melting butter, coconut oil, or chocolate chips; and for my favorite use — cooking polenta (see page 141) without the constant stirring and tending that are required when making it on the cooktop.

MIXING BOWLS: I use glass nesting bowls in small, medium, and large sizes. For mixing bowls, I like Pyrex glass measuring cups (in 4- and 8-cup sizes). These allow me to measure the volume of what I'm cooking and see into the dough from the side of the cup; in addition, the cups are microwave safe.

MUFFIN PANS: A 6-cup standard nonstick (gray, not black) muffin pan is perfect, but you can still use your standard 12-cup muffin pan. Mini-muffin pans are nice for tiny cupcakes or muffins. I specify non stick muffin pans (even if you use paper liners) because they reflect the right amount of heat needed to nicely brown the muffins or cupcakes. This in turn forms a crust or structure that encourages rising, resulting in a prettier and more thoroughly-cooked baked item. I buy these pans in my local grocery store under the brands of Baker's Secret and Good Cook. While you might read that you need to add water to the unused cups on a muffin pan, experts say this step is unnecessary.

PIE PANS: I find that 6-inch pie pans are perfect for small pies. I prefer the nonstick (gray, not black) version because it browns the underside of

the pie crust better, but use what you can find. The small pie pans also work great for quiches and some main dishes.

PORTABLE ELECTRIC MIXER: Don't get rid of your stand mixer, which will come in handy if you make a standard-size loaf of bread, but a portable or handheld mixer is all you will need for the recipes in this book. Choose a sturdy model from a name brand such as KitchenAid, which will last longer than the ultra-cheap versions. You will be using this appliance often, so you want it to last.

POTS, PANS, AND BOWLS: Cooking for two means you will need some new pots and pans or to use your old pans in new ways. It is essential to have the right equipment on hand if you're cooking small.

For example, a 12-inch skillet completely overwhelms the two boneless pork chops that an 8- or 10-inch skillet more effectively accommodates. A 6-inch skillet is better when frying eggs for two. When baking for two, a 6-inch cake pan accommodates a small cake quite nicely, while a 3¼x5¾-inch mini-loaf pan is perfect for quick breads such as cornbread.

I could go on and on, but you get the idea: Smaller is better; in fact, it is imperative. If you already own larger equipment, donate it or store it away for those times when you cook for larger groups, and keep these preferred pots, pans, and skillets available. But don't let this seemingly extensive list deter you from cooking small; add new pieces as you need them rather than all at once.

POTS AND SAUCEPANS: You can put away your big Dutch ovens. I use a 3-quart Emerilware pot for boiling pasta, making certain soups, making broths, and so on. My 2-quart All-Clad saucepan (6-inches in diameter; 4⅛-inches tall) gets used every day in my kitchen for many entrées. All-Clad lasts a lifetime, but there are many good but less expensive brands available that would also work well. In my recipes, I am careful to specify the exact pan size because if you use a pan that is too wide, sauce spreads out too much and evaporates more quickly, making the dish drier. I also prefer glass lids so I can see what's happening without lifting the lid.

RAMEKINS: Small-batch cooking just naturally lends itself to individualized portions, baked in appropriate-sized ramekins. Ramekins are small dishes — usually holding one serving — but there are many different sizes of ramekins, and their size is not always clearly labeled on the ramekin. I try to specify the correct size for each recipe, but you will mostly be using 4-ounce ramekins that have 3¼-inch diameters and 1¾-inch sides. A slightly larger 6-ounce version measures 3½ inches with 2-inch sides, and there are 8-ounce sizes with 4-inch diameters. If you're in doubt about the size of a ramekin, fill it with water to within ¼ inch of the top, and then measure the water in a measuring cup to determine the number of ounces it holds. You can find ramekins in grocery stores, kitchen stores, and online.

ROASTING PAN: Although I like pan-roasting in small skillets without a lid, a small lidded roasting pan can be used for roasting a whole chicken (if you're having guests) or braising entrées in the oven. I use a 12-inch, lidded Granite-Ware roasting pan that I've had forever that roasts evenly and perfectly.

SLOW COOKER: My 4-quart slow cooker works for all my small-batch recipes, but a 2-quart size will also work for most recipes in this book. For easier cleaning, make sure the stoneware pot is removable. If not, you can use disposable liners.

SKILLETS (NONSTICK AND REGULAR): I use 6- and 8-inch nonstick skillets, and occasionally a 10-inch (for especially large, flat cuts of meat, such as flank or skirt steak). A cast-iron version comes in handy, as well. Glass lids are useful here, too.

> *You may wonder why I often specify "gray, not black" for nonstick baking pans. Gray nonstick baking pans provide just the right amount of browning but are not as likely to burn your baked goods as black nonstick pans, so gray is better. However, I don't recommend nonstick baking sheets for baking cookies because they may burn on the bottom.*

TOASTER OVEN: Many gluten-free kitchens have a toaster oven on the countertop. Its primary use is for toasting bread and quick heating jobs — and it is especially good at preventing cross-contamination if it's only used for gluten-free food. But it is also perfect for baking small casseroles. The recipes in this book use a standard oven, but feel free to use your toaster oven if you have one. Mine is a very simple model that takes up minimal space on the countertop. Super-fancy versions are not necessary.

Special Utensils

Your spatulas, stirring spoons, cutting boards, and instant-read thermometers are fine for small-batch cooking. You will also need small-size storage containers for unused ingredients that will be used in later meals, and knives. (Regarding knives, all you really need is a well-sharpened chef's knife, a paring knife, and a serrated knife.) Here are the other utensils that are useful in a small-batch kitchen.

MEASURING SPOON SET: This is one utensil that requires special attention in small-batch cooking. First, be sure to use standardized measuring spoons, not teaspoons from the silverware drawer. It is essential that you measure correctly because in a small recipe, the margin of error is so minute.

For example, a difference of just 1 tablespoon of milk or water can mean the difference between cake batter that is too wet, too dry, or just right because that single tablespoon is a larger percentage of the overall volume than with a larger recipe.

In many small-batch recipes, you will see very small measurements (such as ¹⁄₁₆ or ¹⁄₃₂ teaspoon) and terms such as a *pinch, dash,* and *smidgen*. Here is what those terms mean:

> TAD = ¼ teaspoon
> DASH = ⅛ teaspoon
> PINCH = ¹⁄₁₆ teaspoon
> SMIDGEN = ¹⁄₃₂ teaspoon
> DROP = ¹⁄₆₄ teaspoon

To measure these small amounts correctly, invest in a set of mini-measuring spoons that are available in grocery stores, kitchen shops, and online. For some reason, the spoons are labeled with the word (e.g., *dash*) rather than the numerical fraction (⅛ teaspoon) so I list both measurements in the recipes for the amounts of ⅛, ¹⁄₁₆, ¹⁄₃₂, and ¹⁄₆₄.

One final word on utensils such as measuring spoons: When you are preparing gluten-free food, you must avoid cross-contamination; always thoroughly wash utensils used with gluten-containing food before using them for gluten-free food.

PASTRY BRUSH: Cross-contamination is especially likely with a traditional pastry brush, with its many hair-like strands. For that reason, I only use silicone pastry brushes, which are much easier to clean and just as effective. If you prefer traditional pastry brushes, label one for gluten-free food and another for gluten-containing food (if both are prepared in your kitchen). Find them in grocery stores, kitchen stores, and online.

TOASTER BAGS: Okay, these are not really a kitchen utensil. They are nonstick reusable bags to enclose your gluten-free bread when toasting in a non-dedicated toaster. The bags are perfect for traveling. But I also use them to make grilled-cheese sandwiches at home. You simply insert your assembled sandwich into the bag and drop it into a wide-slot toaster. The bread toasts and the cheese melts — simultaneously — giving you a quick sandwich without using a skillet or buttering the toast. Of course, you have to wipe out melted cheese from inside the bag, but that is easy to do. You can find toaster bags in grocery stores, natural food stores, and online.

Right-Size Shopping for the Small-Batch Kitchen

Although shopping in bulk can save you money, a more conservative approach works best for small-batch, gluten-free kitchens. A small cost savings per ounce or pound means little when you're purchasing more food than you can reasonably use, which can result in food waste. In addition, gluten-free shoppers should avoid bulk bins — especially in areas that contain products with gluten such as flours, grains, and seeds — because of the possibility of cross-contamination.

So, it is better for gluten-free, small-batch cooks to buy smaller sizes, when possible, or consider my suggestions that follow. Here are some ingredients that deserve special consideration in small-batch kitchens.

BREAD CRUMBS: You can buy gluten-free bread crumbs, but you can also make your own easily. They are fresher, taste better, and you can make as much (or as little) as you need (see Homemade Gluten-Free Bread Crumbs on page 127) without having a large store-bought package sitting in your pantry forever.

CANNED GOODS: When possible, choose smaller cans. For example, 8-ounce cans of fruit such as pineapple or peaches are better for two people than the 14-ounce size. Yes, they cost more per ounce, but unless you are sure you will use up the leftovers or your recipe specifies the larger can, buy the smaller version. For other canned goods such as broth or beans, buy 14-ounce cans; leftovers keep well in the refrigerator, and you will most likely use most or all of each can.

FRESH HERBS: For most recipes, fresh herbs are better than dried, but there are certainly some recipes (such as slow-cooker dishes) that are better with dried herbs because fresh ones lose their punch during prolonged cooking. If you are left with a half-used quantity of fresh herbs, consider freezing them. I freeze parsley, cilantro, dill, and rosemary in small plastic bags with success while other cooks toss the chopped herbs in olive oil and freeze in ice-cube trays. The herbs won't be crisp and green when thawed, but once they are in a pot of soup or stew, it doesn't matter. I also dry leftover fresh herbs in the microwave oven, nestled in a dry paper towel, until they are completely dehydrated.

FRUITS AND VEGETABLES: For perishables, if you don't want to buy whole quantities of salad greens and fresh fruits and vegetables, consider the salad bar at your local grocery store or deli. Make sure the bar is cleanly kept with high turnover, assuring you that everything is fresh; then use what you buy soon after you bring it home. Per pound, these items may be

more expensive, but you won't be left with spoiled leftovers that end up being thrown away. It is also a good place to buy cherry tomatoes, olives, and (gluten-free) salad dressings in small quantities.

Some grocery stores accommodate small households in the produce section. For example, I can buy individual carrots (rather than a whole bag) and individual stalks of celery (rather than the whole bunch). Potatoes and onions are sold individually, rather than in large bags. Also, packages of mixed, pre-cut stir-fry veggies may work for you if they contain a little bit of several different kinds of vegetables that fit into the recipes you plan to prepare.

ONION AND OTHER SMALL-QUANTITY INGREDIENTS: Of course, you can always use fresh onion in any recipe. But for small households it seems silly to haul out a big onion only to chop 1 tablespoon for your small-scale recipe. In that event, do as I often do, and use an equivalent amount of dried minced onion. It keeps on your pantry shelf for a long time and adds that unmistakable onion flavor with little effort from you. I also keep dried celery flakes and dried green bell pepper in the pantry for the same reason. I always prefer the flavor of fresh vegetables, but I love the convenience of dried versions. In this same vein, you can use garlic powder or jarred garlic, although fresh garlic cloves are usually better.

TOMATO PASTE: Certain condiments, such as tomato paste, anchovy paste, and pesto, are better bought in tubes rather than cans or jars. You can use as little as you like (the 1 tablespoon of tomato paste in some of my recipes adds remarkable flavor) and you can put the tube back in the refrigerator for another time.

Baking Ingredients

Some ingredients require special attention in the small-batch kitchen, especially in baking. It is easy to measure 2 tablespoons of milk, or a tablespoon of cornstarch, but the following ingredients merit some discussion.

EGGS: Scaling down a four-serving recipe to feed only two people is not as easy as dividing each ingredient by two. Because of this, one of the most confounding ingredients in baking is eggs. Measuring one-third of an egg (or some similar fraction) is very hard. So, I never use less than 1 large egg in a baked item. But this means I had to make adjustments in other ingredients to account for the liquid (about 3 tablespoons) that each large egg contains. When I developed these recipes I didn't want to make you buy liquid eggs in a container and then tediously measure fractions of whole eggs; I thought it easier for you to use a whole large egg and for me to make other adjustments in the recipe.

FATS, OILS, AND BUTTER: Fat is a critical component in baking and real butter lends that unmistakable wonderful flavor, so buy your favorite brand in quantities that suit your needs. Butter freezes well, so buy the pound box of four sticks and thaw the sticks as you need them. But if dairy is a problem you can use a soy or rice-based buttery spread (such as Earth Balance) in place of butter. If a recipe calls for unsalted butter and you use buttery spread (which contains salt) you may want to decrease the salt in the recipe by 25 percent to compensate for the salt in the spread.

For oil in baking, I usually use canola oil (use organic if you are concerned about GMOs) or vegetable oil, but you may also use coconut oil (melted before measuring), grapeseed oil, rice bran oil, or whatever oil you prefer.

LEAVENING: Leavening is critical in gluten-free baking because it makes baked goods rise. Make sure your yeast, baking powder, and baking soda are fresh by checking the expiration labels. Unless you bake a lot, buy these leavening agents in the smallest quantities possible so you use them up before they expire. Buy yeast in the individual packets (rather than jars or tubs) and store it in the refrigerator or freezer to prolong its life.

MILK: Feel free to use your favorite cow's milk in these recipes and buy in quantities that suit your needs. I used 1% cow's milk during testing because that is what most people use. But an inability to digest cow's milk often accompanies gluten intolerance and a huge percentage (some estimates are as high as 60 percent, but it varies by ethnic group) of Americans are dairy-intolerant. Feel free to use your favorite nondairy beverage in place of cow's milk. I am fond of the lactose-free versions of milk, yogurt, cream cheese, kefir, and sour cream from Green Valley Organics. For nondairy beverages, my advice is to avoid the unsweetened versions for baking because they don't have enough sugar to mimic cow's milk. Avoid vanilla-flavored varieties in savory dishes because they taste weird. My favorite nondairy milk for baking is Living Harvest Tempt hemp milk (original flavor), but I also use various brands of plain almond, soy, rice, and coconut milk. Each has a unique flavor and texture, so experiment to find the one you like.

SALT: Salt does wonders for the taste of food, but I am leery of over-salting. For example, a full-salt chicken broth makes a saltier soup than a low-sodium version. For that reason, I use the bare minimum of salt in each recipe, but also suggest — in certain recipes — that you taste the dish just before serving to see if it needs more salt. Remember, you can always add more salt but it is very hard to salvage an over-salted dish. For these recipes I used sea salt, but you can also use table salt. Coarse kosher doesn't dissolve well in baking, so I don't use it.

XANTHAN GUM: My recipes are formulated with my customized flour blend that sometimes requires a small amount of xanthan gum (or you can use guar gum, if you wish) for the best baking results. I try to use the smallest amount possible only in those recipes that truly need it, and if a recipe calls for a gum, you do need to use it for the recipe to come out correctly. If you are allergic or intolerant to gums, some of the recipes in this book will not be appropriate for you.

Gluten-Free Flours and Flour Blends

The recipes in this book rely on my own carefully crafted gluten-free flour blend, an extremely versatile blend that can be used as the basis for many dishes so you don't have to store lots of different flours in your small pantry. I use this blend because it is made up of flours that are most common in gluten-free kitchens, plus they are mild in flavor and among the least costly of all gluten-free flours.

For my blend, I use brown rice flour as the main flour, but if you want more protein and fiber in your diet, you may replace it with sorghum flour. Your baked goods will be a bit darker in color and slightly denser in texture, but delicious nonetheless.

I prepare this flour blend ahead of time and store it on my pantry shelf in a food-safe container from the Container Store. Because the recipe makes 4 cups — and most baking recipes use about ½ cup — it will last you for a while, depending on how often you bake.

Flours will also be the basis for thickening your food. For savory gravies and sauces, I prefer sweet rice flour, which is not the same as regular white or brown rice flour. Sweet rice flour is made from the sweet, sticky rice served in Asian restaurants and yields the closest thing to a wheat-thickened sauce in appearance and texture. It is somewhat opaque and not shiny, like a cornstarch-thickened sauce. It is available in natural food stores and online.

For dessert, and especially fruit desserts, I prefer either cornstarch or tapioca flour/starch or potato starch because they produce a somewhat shiny, transparent sauce that enhances the appearance of fruit. In all of my recipes, I specify my preferred thickener. Arrowroot is also a nice thickener for some desserts and gives a nice sheen to the finished dish.

I use standard brands of flours purchased in natural food stores or supermarkets. My recipes were tested with Bob's Red Mill flours. I don't use super-fine flours, such as those from Asian markets, because they absorb

Carol's Gluten-Free Flour Blend

1½ cups brown rice flour (or sorghum flour)

1½ cups potato starch (or cornstarch or arrowroot)

1 cup tapioca flour/starch

Makes 4 cups. Whisk the ingredients together until well blended. Store, tightly covered, in a dark, dry place for up to two weeks. If you refrigerate or freeze the blend for longer-term storage up to 3 months, bring it to room temperature before using. You may double or triple the recipe, if you wish.

liquids differently than the standard brands. I don't grind my own flours because I need the consistency of store-bought flours to make sure the recipe works the same way each and every time.

IT IS VERY IMPORTANT TO MEASURE FLOUR CAREFULLY: Whisk the flour a few times to aerate or fluff it up, and then lightly spoon it into a measuring cup before leveling it off with a knife. Don't use the measuring cup as a scoop and don't pack the flour down; scooping will give you 20 percent more flour than spooning, which can cause recipe failure. Use spouted measuring cups only for liquids because it's hard to determine an accurate amount of flour in them. To see flour measured, see videos at CarolFenster.com.

Savvy Label Reading

It is very important to choose gluten-free ingredients carefully. The Food Allergen Labeling and Consumer Protection Act of 2004 (FALCPA) makes

shopping easier because the words "Contains: Wheat" must appear on any food that contains wheat. Re-read the labels each time you buy a product, though, because manufacturers can change procedures or ingredients at any time. Also, the law only requires the warning about wheat, not the other gluten-containing grains such as barley, rye, spelt, kamut, and triticale —but these ingredients will be in the ingredient list so you will know if that food is safe or not.

In 2014, the Food and Drug Administration defined "gluten-free" as a product with "less than 20 parts per million (ppm) of gluten." There is no requirement that gluten-free foods carry a gluten-free label, but when a manufacturer chooses to put the words *gluten-free* on food packaging, the item must comply with the FDA definition. As long as the final food product contains less than 20 ppm gluten, it can carry a gluten-free label — even if some of the individual ingredients test higher than 20 ppm. I know this sounds confusing, but that's how this definition plays out. It means that manufacturers may use previously banned ingredients, such as regular oats or wheat starch, in their formulas as long as the finished product tests below 20 ppm. This means you have to decide for yourself whether to eat these products.

To further help you identify safe foods, the Gluten-Free Certification Organization (a branch of the Gluten Intolerance Group) certifies companies as gluten-free and authorizes them to display a certification logo on the food item. The Celiac Sprue Association and the National Foundation for Celiac Awareness also offer certification programs. Companies that don't use these logos don't necessarily manufacture unsafe foods, but these logos are yet another tool for you to use when you shop.

About the Recipes

Kinds of Recipes in this Book

How did I select the recipes that appear in this book? For the entrées, I focused on family favorites that we all grew up with, like meat loaf and tuna-noodle casserole. I took suggestions from people who emailed me or asked me questions at conferences, trade shows, and speaking engagements. I looked for world cuisine and diversity across ethnic dishes (Italian, Asian, Mexican), cuts of meat (ground beef, chicken parts, chops, steaks), and flavor intensity (mild to bold). For desserts, I chose the basics that we all miss on a gluten-free diet like cakes, cookies, and pies. Finally, like a lot of cookbook authors, I chose recipes that I like to eat. Hopefully, you will too.

I tried to write these recipes with you in mind: how you organize your kitchen, how you shop for food, and how you store it. For example, I try to be as specific as possible when I list certain ingredients (such as grated cheese) that are purchased by weight. Because most of you do not own kitchen scales, however, I list both weight (2 ounces) and volume (½ cup) for those types of ingredients.

For vegetarians, I include a (v) icon at recipes that are vegetarian. I also provide cooking times to help you with planning.

Kitchen Math for Two

Cooking involves math, which can be intimidating to some of us. Cooking for two isn't as simple as just dividing ingredient amounts by two, particularly in baking. Just as not all standard recipes can be scaled up to feed a crowd, many recipes are destined for outright failure if they're pared down to small sizes. So this book is about helping you enjoy your favorite gluten-free foods in small-batch sizes, where the downsizing is already done for you.

You already know how to fry two pork chops, bake two potatoes, or grill two hamburgers, so in this book I focus on more complex recipes that required kitchen math and additional finagling on my part to create workable recipes. In the recipes that follow, you will find the dishes that required more than just arithmetic (as in reducing a multi-ingredient, four-serving recipe down to two servings), such as casseroles, sauced dishes, and baked goods.

Yields

The recipes in this book are designed to serve two people, so most main dish recipes yield two servings. The baking recipes, however, bring up an interesting conundrum in serving sizes. For example, you will notice that some of the muffin and cake recipes make four servings, while others make six. The cookie recipes make from four to twelve cookies, while the cakes yield slightly different sizes.

The reason for this inconsistency in servings is that combinations of ingredients in baking require exact proportions to rise properly. Different ingredients absorb liquids at different rates. And, because I didn't want to use fractions of eggs, which would require tedious measuring, most recipes use whole eggs. So, to achieve the right proportions of ingredients for a successful dish, some recipes differ in yield from most others. Compared to the standard recipes for four people, however, all yields in this book are still considered small.

Leftovers

Even though I try hard to avoid unnecessary extra ingredients in these recipes, some leftovers are bound to happen. You'll see that at the end of some recipes I offer suggestions for how to use these leftovers in other ways.

Nutrition Information

Many people want to know what's in their food (such as calories, fat, protein, fiber, sodium, cholesterol, carbohydrates, and so on) and how the analysis was calculated. I used nutritional software called MasterCook Deluxe to do these calculations and here is how I handled certain ingredients:

- The first ingredient was used whenever a choice was given (such as unsalted butter or buttery spread; in this case, I used unsalted butter).
- 1% milk was used, unless the recipe specifies otherwise.
- Large eggs were used.

Brands Used in Testing the Recipes

Whenever I write a cookbook, people want to know which brands I used in testing the recipes. Here are the brands I used, but listing these ingredients is not an endorsement of these companies. These ingredients were gluten free at the time of testing, but you should always read labels before buying any food or ingredient to make sure it is gluten free. Manufacturers can change ingredients or manufacturing practices, making a formerly gluten-free product no longer safe. Also, some manufacturers use similar packaging for their gluten and gluten-free products, so reading the labels is necessary to distinguish between the two. And, some companies may go out of business or change their names after this book was printed.

Baking and Cooking Ingredients

- Chocolate chips: Tropical Source/ Sunspire, Enjoy Life mini chocolate chips, or Ghirardelli
- Chocolate cookies: Pamela's dark chocolate chunk
- Cocoa powder (unsweetened, natural): Hershey's; (Dutch, alkali): Callebaut
- Cookie crumbs: Pamela's cookies
- Milk powder substitute: Better Than Milk soy powder
- Shortening (non-hydrogenated): Spectrum, Earth Balance, or Crisco
- Xanthan gum: Bob's Red Mill

Beverages, Drinks

- Coffee liqueur: Kahlúa

Bread, Tortillas, Chips, Crackers

- Bread, cinnamon-raisin: Udi's
- Bread, sandwich: Rudi's Gluten-Free Bakery, Udi's, Whole Foods, and Canyon Bakehouse
- Bread crumbs: Kinnikinnick or Hol-Grain
- Polenta tube: Food Merchants (Ancient Harvest)
- Taco shells, corn: Garden of Eatin'
- Tortillas, corn: Mission Foods
- Tortillas, flour: Rudi's, Food for Life, or La Tortilla Factory
- Tortilla chips, corn: Mission Foods
- Wraps: Toufayan

Candy, Cookies, Desserts, Toppings, Sauces

- Cookies: Pamela's
- Chocolate syrup: Hershey's
- Graham crackers: Pamela's
- Whipped topping: Lucerne or Soyatoo

Condiments, Savory Sauces, Dips

- Artichokes, marinated: Mezzetta
- Asian seasoning: Spice Island garam masala or McCormick Perfect Pinch Asian seasoning
- Barbecue sauce: Cattlemen's or Heinz Original
- Bouillon powder: Orrington Farms

- Cajun seasoning: McCormick Pinch Perfect, Spice Islands (salt-free)
- Chili sauce: Heinz
- Chipotle chili pepper powder: McCormick
- Cocktail sauce: Heinz
- Curry paste, green: A Taste of Thai
- Curry paste, red: A Taste of Thai
- Enchilada sauce: Las Palmas or La Victoria
- Fish sauce: A Taste of Thai or Thai Kitchen
- Hoisin sauce: Premier Japan
- Hot pepper sauce: Tabasco or Frank's RedHot
- Jam, raspberry: Bonne Maman
- Marinara sauce: Classico or Prego
- Mayonnaise alternative: Just Mayo
- Mayonnaise substitute/salad dressing: Miracle Whip or Just Mayo
- (Eastern) Mediterranean-style seasoning: McCormick or Lawry's Seasoned Salt with Mediterranean herbs
- Montreal steak seasoning: McCormick Grill Mates
- Mustard, Dijon: Grey Poupon
- Mustard, ground: McCormick
- Onion, dried minced: Kroger
- Onion powder: McCormick
- Salsa, Mexican: Mission, Tostito, Newman's Own, La Victoria, Pace, or Herdez traditional
- Salsa verde, Mexican: La Victoria or Herdez
- Seafood seasoning: Spice Islands Grilling Gourmet Spicy Seafood Seasoning or Old Bay
- Seasoned salt: Lawry's

- Southwest seasoning: McCormick Perfect Pinch
- Tamari (gluten-free soy sauce): San-J or Kikkoman
- Teriyaki sauce: Premier Japan
- Tofu, soft silken: Mori-Nu
- Worcestershire sauce: French's or Lea & Perrins (in the U.S., not in Canada)

Dairy, Cheese, Tofu

- Buttery spread: Earth Balance
- Cheese alternatives: Vegan Gourmet or Daiya
    - cheddar: Daiya
    - cream cheese : Tofutti, Vegan Gourmet, or Green Valley Organics
    - mozzarella: Daiya
    - Monterey Jack: Daiya
    - Parmesan: Go Veggie
    - Swiss: Daiya
- Ice cream: Ben & Jerry's or Häagen-Dazs
- Kefir: Green Valley Organics
- Milk alternatives:
    - almond: Silk
    - coconut: So Delicious
    - flaxseed: Good Karma
    - hazelnut: Pacific Natural Foods
    - hemp: Living Harvest Tempt
    - rice: Rice Dream
    - soy: Silk
- Milk powder: Organic Valley
- Milk powder substitute: Better Than Milk
- Sour cream alternative: Tofutti, Vegan Gourmet, or Green Valley Organics
- Tofu, soft silken: Moni-Nu
- Whipped cream or whipped topping: Lucerne or Soyatoo

- Yogurt, lactose-free: Green Valley Organics

Flours, Grains

- Almond meal/flour: Bob's Red Mill or Honeyville Farms
- Chia seeds: Bob's Red Mill (brown/black) or Nutiva (white/tan)
- Corn grits (polenta): Bob's Red Mill
- Cornmeal: Bob's Red Mill
- Flaxseed meal: Bob's Red Mill
- Hazelnut meal/flour: Bob's Red Mill
- Oats, gluten-free (quick-cooking, rolled, steel-cut): Bob's Red Mill
- Polenta tube: Food Merchants (Ancient Harvest)
- Potato starch: Bob's Red Mill
- Quinoa: Bob's Red Mill
- Rice, brown: Bob's Red Mill
- Rice, white long-grain: Bob's Red Mill
- Rice, wild: Lundberg
- Sorghum flour: Bob's Red Mill or Shiloh Farms
- Sorghum grain: Bob's Red Mill
- Sweet rice flour: Bob's Red Mill
- Tapioca flour: Bob's Red Mill

Meats

- Chorizo: Johnsonville
- Sausage, andouille: Applegate or Johnsonville
- Sausage, Italian: Applegate or Boulder Sausage
- Pepperoni slices: Hormel

Pasta

- Elbow macaroni: Tinkyáda or Barilla
- Egg noodles: Jovial
- Fettuccine: Tinkyáda or DeBoles
- Lasagna: Tinkyáda or DeBoles
- Penne: Tinkyáda, Schär, or Barilla
- Spaghetti: Tinkyáda or Barilla
- Spiral pasta: Tinkyáda or Barilla

Soups

- Bouillon powder or cubes: Herb-Ox, or Lee Kum Kee
- Broth, beef: Swanson's (low sodium)
- Broth, chicken: Swanson's Natural Goodness (low sodium)
- Broth, vegetarian: Imagine No-Chicken

Vegetables (Canned or Frozen)

- Frozen hash browns: Ore-Ida
- Mexican-style tomatoes: Ro-Tel

For More Information on Avoiding Gluten

This is a cookbook about preparing meals but if you need more information about the various medical conditions that require a gluten-free diet, see Sources at the end of this book.

Breakfast & Brunch

Breakfast is my favorite meal

of the day, so I never skip it. Like you, I can handle pouring cereal into the bowl, frying an egg, or making toast for two people. But what about breakfast casseroles, pancakes, waffles, or other dishes that have multiple ingredients? How do you scale all those ingredients down to two servings? Kitchen math, too early in the morning!

In this chapter I've taken a wide variety of recipes that are most likely to confound the two-person household and done the math for you.

To further simplify the morning routine, in many of the baked items you can mix the dry ingredients together the night before; likewise for the wet ingredients. Just don't mix them together until morning (unless the recipe says otherwise) or they won't rise properly.

I've included a lot of baked recipes in this chapter, but be sure to check out the Breads chapter (page 152) for even more delicious baked goods to enjoy in the morning.

Pancakes

Ⓥ

What would weekends be without pancakes? But if you want them during the week and don't have lots of time in the morning, mix up the batter ahead of time and refrigerate for up to 2 days—making it easy to have pancakes anytime, with little effort. Squeeze a drop of lemon juice into the batter to revive it just before frying.

MAKES 2 SERVINGS
(THREE 4-INCH
PANCAKES EACH)

1 cup Carol's Gluten-Free
Flour Blend (page 24)

1 tablespoon granulated
sugar

1 teaspoon baking
powder

¼ teaspoon salt

⅛ teaspoon (dash)
baking soda

1 large egg

⅓ to ½ cup milk of
choice

2 tablespoons unsalted
butter, melted and
slightly cooled,
or canola oil, plus more
for the pan

Toppings of choice:
maple syrup, honey,
jelly, jam, nut butter,
fresh fruit

1. In a blender, blend all ingredients except the toppings, starting with ⅓ cup milk; add more milk, a tablespoon at a time, to reach a thick yet pourable consistency. Alternately, whisk the ingredients together in a small bowl. Let the batter stand for 5 minutes while preheating the skillet or griddle to medium heat.

2. Lightly oil a 10-inch nonstick skillet and heat over medium heat. Use a ¼-cup dry measuring cup to portion the batter. First scoop out a test pancake and cook until the top is bubbly, 3 to 5 minutes, to judge if the pan is too hot, not hot enough, or just right. If the pancake doesn't bubble soon enough or too soon, adjust the heat under the skillet. Turn and cook until golden brown, 2 to 3 minutes longer. If you find the batter is thicker than you like, add more milk, a tablespoon at a time, to get a more pourable consistency.

3. Continue cooking the pancakes, three at a time. Serve immediately with your favorite toppings.

Per pancake: 150 calories; 2g protein; 4g total fat; 1g fiber;
23g carbohydrates; 42mg cholesterol; 214mg sodium

Gingerbread Pancakes ⓥ

The warming spices in this pancake are perfect for a cold fall morning. Serve with pumpkin butter or apple butter . . . or a drizzle of maple syrup.

MAKES 2 SERVINGS
(THREE 4-INCH
PANCAKES EACH)

1 cup Carol's Gluten-Free Flour Blend (page 24)

1 teaspoon pumpkin pie spice

1 teaspoon baking powder

⅛ teaspoon (dash) baking soda

⅛ teaspoon (dash) salt

½ cup buttermilk or plain kefir (or Homemade Buttermilk, below), plus more if needed

1 large egg

1½ tablespoons molasses

1 tablespoon canola oil, plus more for the pan

Toppings of choice: maple syrup, honey, jelly, jam, nut butter, fresh fruit

1. In a small bowl, whisk together the flour blend, pumpkin pie spice, baking powder, baking soda, and salt until well blended. Whisk in the ½ cup of buttermilk, egg, molasses, and oil until smooth. Let the batter stand for 5 minutes.

2. Lightly oil a 10-inch nonstick skillet and heat over medium heat. Using a ¼-cup dry measuring cup to portion the batter, first scoop out a test pancake and cook until the top is bubbly, 3 to 5 minutes. If the pancake doesn't bubble soon enough or too soon, adjust the heat under the skillet. Turn the pancake and cook until golden brown, 2 to 3 minutes longer. If you find the batter is thicker than you like, add more buttermilk, a tablespoon at a time, to get a more pourable consistency.

3. Continue cooking the pancakes, three at a time. Serve immediately with your favorite toppings.

HOMEMADE BUTTERMILK To make homemade buttermilk, stir 1 teaspoon apple cider vinegar into ½ cup dairy or nondairy milk. Let stand 5 minutes without stirring again, and then use in your recipe.

LEFTOVER PANCAKES If you have leftover pancakes, wrap them lightly in foil and refrigerate for up to 3 days. To eat later, remove the foil and warm gently on Low in the microwave.

Per pancake: 145 calories; 2g protein; 4g total fat; 1g fiber; 25g carbohydrates; 42mg cholesterol; 188mg sodium

Preparation time: 5 minutes
Chilling time: 1 hour
Cooking time: 5 minutes

Crepes

(V)

*Crepes can be enjoyed as both a main dish and dessert, and this versatile recipe
works both ways. On weekends, fill them with scrambled eggs for breakfast
or brunch. For dessert, roll up with chocolate-hazelnut spread or a fruit filling
such as cherry pie filling—or fold in quarters and top with raspberry jam and a
dusting of powdered sugar. A drizzle of chocolate syrup isn't bad, either!*

MAKES 2 SERVINGS
(2 CREPES EACH)

⅓ cup Carol's Gluten-
Free Flour Blend
(page 24)

⅛ teaspoon (dash)
granulated sugar

¹⁄₁₆ teaspoon (pinch) salt

⅓ cup milk of choice

1 large egg, at room
temperature

1 tablespoon melted
unsalted butter or
buttery spread

Additional butter,
buttery spread, or canola
oil for greasing the pan

Toppings of choice:
chocolate syrup, honey,
jelly, jam, powdered
sugar

Fillings of choice:
chocolate-hazelnut
spread, nut butter,
pie filling, jelly, jam,
scrambled eggs, or
cooked meat, fish, or
poultry

1. Put all of the ingredients except the grease for the pan,
   toppings or filling in a blender and process until the
   mixture is smooth. Refrigerate 1 hour. Just before cooking
   the crepes, blend again to reincorporate ingredients.

2. Heat an 8-inch skillet or seasoned crepe pan over
   medium-high heat until a drop of water dances on the
   surface.

3. For each crepe, brush the surface of the skillet with
   butter. Pour a scant ¼ cup batter into the pan and
   immediately tilt and swirl the pan to coat the bottom
   evenly with crepe batter. Cook until the underside of the
   crepe browns, about 2 to 3 minutes. Flip the crepe with a
   thin spatula and cook the other side for 20 to 30 seconds,
   or until the crepe batter sets. You may need to adjust the
   temperature of the burner to maintain the right heat.

4. Stack the cooked crepes between sheets of foil
   or parchment paper to prevent drying out. Serve
   immediately with your preferred toppings and/or fillings.

CREPE SHAPES When I make crepes, I use a very old, well-
seasoned 6½-inch crepe pan with sloping sides. The
¼ cup of batter fills the entire bottom of this pan, creating
a perfectly round crepe. If you use a larger skillet, the batter
may not spread evenly, creating a less-than-round crepe
with irregular edges. Don't worry; this irregularity is not
noticeable when the crepe is rolled up.

Per serving: 180 calories; 6g protein; 9g total fat; 1g fiber;
19g carbohydrates; 111mg cholesterol; 116mg sodium

Waffles

ⓥ

To me, waffles are special and a little more involved than pancakes, but are still a wonderful choice when cooking for two. Feel free to top yours creatively; anything goes when it comes to waffles!

MAKES 2 SERVINGS,
½ (8-INCH) BELGIAN
WAFFLE EACH

1 cup Carol's Gluten-Free Flour Blend (page 24)

1 tablespoon granulated sugar

1 teaspoon baking powder

⅛ teaspoon (dash) baking soda

⅛ teaspoon (dash) salt

1 large egg, separated

⅓ cup buttermilk, plain kefir, or Homemade Buttermilk (page 37)

½ teaspoon pure vanilla extract

2 tablespoons unsalted butter or buttery spread, melted and cooled, or canola oil

Toppings of choice: maple syrup, honey, jelly, jam, nut butter, fresh fruit

1. Preheat a waffle iron according to the manufacturer's directions.

2. In a medium bowl, whisk together the flour blend, sugar, baking powder, baking soda, and salt until well blended. In a separate small bowl, beat the egg white with an electric mixer on medium-low speed until stiff peaks form. In a small measuring cup, whisk together the egg yolk, buttermilk, vanilla, and butter.

3. With an electric mixer on low speed, gently add the egg yolk mixture to the egg white mixture and beat until just combined. Add the flour mixture and beat until just combined. The batter should be fairly thick, yet thin enough to spread easily with a spatula on the waffle iron.

4. Coat the waffle iron with cooking spray or lightly grease with oil. Pour the manufacturer's recommended amount of batter onto the heated waffle iron, which will vary depending on the size of your machine. Close and bake until the steaming stops and the waffle is deeply browned, 4 to 6 minutes, depending on your waffle iron. Repeat with remaining batter, if necessary. Serve immediately with your favorite toppings.

HOW BIG ARE THE WAFFLES? I use a Belgian waffle maker, which makes a slightly thicker waffle than traditional waffle irons. So this recipe makes one 8-inch waffle, which is enough for 2 servings. You might get a different number of waffles (and shorter cooking times), depending on the size of your waffle iron.

Per serving: 440 calories; 7g protein; 15g total fat; 3g fiber; 66g carbohydrates; 126mg cholesterol; 571mg sodium

French Toast

French toast is one of my favorite breakfasts. It is a great way to use up stale gluten-free bread, since it is a shame to waste bread of any kind! This recipe is calibrated to make 4 slices. I slather on some butter and maple syrup (or nut butter if I'm feeling the need for protein) and—with a cup of strong coffee— my day is off to a great start!

MAKES 2 SERVINGS
(2 SLICES EACH)

⅓ cup milk of choice

1 large egg, beaten

½ teaspoon pure vanilla extract

½ teaspoon granulated sugar

⅛ teaspoon (dash) ground cinnamon

2 tablespoons unsalted butter or buttery spread, or more as needed

4 slices gluten-free sandwich bread

Toppings of choice: maple syrup, honey, jelly, jam, nut butter, fresh fruit

1. In a wide, shallow bowl, whisk together the milk, egg, vanilla, sugar, and cinnamon until smooth and well blended.

2. In a 10-inch nonstick skillet, heat 1 tablespoon of the butter over medium heat. Dip 2 slices of bread—a slice at a time—into the milk mixture just enough to coat on both sides. Cook in the skillet, turning once, until lightly browned on both sides, 4 to 6 minutes.

3. Heat the remaining 1 tablespoon butter in the skillet and repeat with the remaining 2 slices of bread. Serve immediately with your toppings of choice.

Per serving: 290 calories; 8g protein; 16g total fat; 2g fiber; 29g carbohydrates; 127mg cholesterol; 341mg sodium

Coffee Cake with Streusel

This tasty little cake is wonderful at breakfast—the perfect complement to savory dishes such as eggs and bacon. I bake it as a loaf, rather than a round cake, because it fits perfectly in a 3¼x5¾-inch loaf pan.

MAKES 4 SLICES
(ONE 3¼x5¾-INCH LOAF)

Streusel Topping

1 tablespoon Carol's Gluten-Free Flour Blend (page 24)

1 tablespoon packed brown sugar

1 teaspoon granulated sugar

⅛ teaspoon (dash) ground cinnamon

1½ teaspoons cold unsalted butter or buttery spread

Batter

¾ cup Carol's Gluten-Free Flour Blend (page 24)

⅓ cup granulated sugar

½ teaspoon ground cinnamon

¼ teaspoon xanthan gum

¼ teaspoon baking powder

¼ teaspoon baking soda

¼ teaspoon salt

1 large egg

¼ cup buttermilk, plain kefir, or Homemade Buttermilk (page 37)

2 tablespoons canola oil

½ teaspoon pure vanilla extract

1. Place a rack in the middle of the oven. Preheat the oven to 350°F. Generously grease a 3¼x 5¾-inch nonstick (gray, not black) loaf pan.

2. Make the streusel: In a small bowl, use a fork to whisk together the flour blend, brown sugar, granulated sugar, and cinnamon. Mash in the butter until the topping is crumbly.

3. Make the batter: In a medium bowl, whisk together the flour blend, granulated sugar, cinnamon, xanthan gum, baking powder, baking soda, and salt until well blended. Add the egg, buttermilk, oil, and vanilla and beat with an electric mixer on low speed until well blended, about 1 minute. Spread the batter evenly in the pan. Sprinkle the streusel evenly over the batter and press it lightly into the batter with your fingers.

4. Bake for 30 to 35 minutes, until the top is lightly browned and a toothpick inserted into the center of the cake comes out clean. Cool on a wire rack for 20 minutes before serving.

Per slice: 285 calories; 3g protein; 10g total fat; 2g fiber; 45g carbohydrates; 51mg cholesterol; 290mg sodium

Preparation time: 20 minutes
Chilling time: 1 hour to overnight
Baking time: 35 minutes

Sausage and Egg Strata

This is the perfect dish for weekend brunch. It is especially convenient because you assemble it the night before and then bake it just before serving. For even more flavor, use Italian sausage instead of plain sausage. I make mine in a 4x8-inch Emile Henry ceramic loaf dish and serve it directly from the pan—along with a fruit salad—but it works equally well in a glass loaf pan.

MAKES 2 SERVINGS

3 slices gluten-free sandwich bread, cut into ¾-inch cubes (about 2 cups)

¼ cup sliced mushrooms

4 ounces gluten-free lean sausage (1 link), fully cooked and diced or crumbled

½ cup (2 ounces) shredded mozzarella cheese or cheese alternative, divided

½ cup baby spinach or green peas

¼ cup finely diced yellow onion

2 large eggs

1 cup milk of choice

1 garlic clove, minced

½ teaspoon dried Italian seasoning

¼ teaspoon salt

⅛ teaspoon (dash) freshly ground black pepper

1 tablespoon grated Parmesan cheese or soy Parmesan

1 tablespoon chopped fresh parsley, for garnish

1. Generously grease a 4x8-inch glass or ceramic loaf pan.

2. Place the bread in a medium bowl. Add the mushrooms, sausage, half of the mozzarella, the spinach, and onion and stir together with a spatula. Spread evenly in the baking dish.

3. In a medium bowl, whisk together the eggs, milk, garlic, Italian seasoning, salt, and pepper until thoroughly blended. Pour the mixture evenly over the bread. With a spatula, press on the bread cubes to flatten them a bit and make sure they are fully immersed in the liquid. Tightly cover and refrigerate for at least 1 hour or up to overnight to let the bread soak up the liquids.

4. Place a rack in the middle of the oven. Preheat the oven to 350°F. Uncover the casserole and bake for 30 minutes. Sprinkle with the Parmesan and remaining mozzarella and continue baking until the cheese is melted and browned, about 5 more minutes. Let cool on a wire rack for 10 minutes. Cut and serve, garnished with the parsley.

Per serving: 560 calories; 26g protein; 32g total fat; 2g fiber; 29g carbohydrates; 256mg cholesterol; 1089mg sodium

Kitchen-Sink Hash

Even when you're cooking small meals, those leftovers seem to mysteriously multiply in the fridge. Actually, I sometimes plan to have "dibs-and-dabs" available so I can make hash. It doesn't have to be the usual corned beef version, either. I've used leftover cooked turkey, chicken—even smoked salmon—with excellent results. I also throw in cooked vegetables, such as diced broccoli. Even though eggs aren't typically included in hash, I use two for a little binding effect. (Even with that, I like a fried egg on top, too.) Let your imagination and fridge contents guide what you put into this true kitchen-sink dish!

MAKES 2 SERVINGS

2 tablespoons canola oil

¼ cup diced onion

¼ pound cooked potatoes (small, red, or new potatoes work well), diced

½ pound corned beef or cooked turkey, diced

2 large eggs, beaten

Salt and freshly ground black pepper, to taste

2 fried eggs, for topping (optional)

1 tablespoon chopped fresh parsley, for garnish

⅛ teaspoon (dash) paprika, for garnish

1. In a medium, heavy skillet, heat the oil over medium heat. Add the onion and cook until soft, 3 to 5 minutes. Add the potatoes and cook until the edges begin to brown and become crisp, 2 to 3 minutes. The browner the potatoes, the deeper the overall flavor of the hash. Add the corned beef and continue to cook until the meat is heated through, about 2 minutes.

2. Pour the beaten eggs over the hash and continue to cook, stirring until they reach your desired doneness, 1 to 2 minutes.

3. Taste and add salt and pepper to taste. Serve, topped with a fried egg (if you like) and garnished with parsley and paprika.

Per serving: 460 calories; 23g protein; 35g total fat; 1g fiber; 13g carbohydrates; 248mg cholesterol; 198mg sodium

Herb Frittata

(V)

Here is another dish that uses up leftover cooked potatoes—or pasta or vegetables if you like. In spring, try parboiled asparagus bits. In summer, zucchini is nice. Or add chopped marinated artichokes or roasted red peppers from a jar. While a frittata is traditional for breakfast, it also makes a quick, light dinner.

MAKES 2 SERVINGS

4 large eggs

¼ cup chopped fresh herbs, such as parsley or chives, plus extra for garnish

2 tablespoons grated Parmesan cheese or soy Parmesan, plus extra for garnish

⅛ teaspoon (dash) salt

⅛ teaspoon (dash) freshly ground black pepper

1 tablespoon unsalted butter, buttery spread, or canola oil

¾ cup diced cooked potatoes, pasta, or vegetables

2 tablespoons shredded mozzarella or other cheese of choice

1. Preheat the broiler and place a rack 6 inches from the heat.

2. In a small bowl, whisk the eggs, herbs, Parmesan, salt, and pepper until well blended. In an 8-inch ovenproof skillet, heat the butter over medium heat. Add the egg mixture and potatoes and cook, while tilting the pan to distribute the uncooked egg evenly and using a spatula to lift the cooked edges and let the uncooked egg flow underneath. Cook for 3 to 5 minutes, until the egg begins to firm up. Sprinkle with the mozzarella.

3. Place the skillet on the rack in the oven and broil just until the eggs are set to your liking and the cheese is melted, about 30 seconds. Cut in half and serve immediately, garnished with herbs and a sprinkle of Parmesan.

Per serving: 275 calories; 16g protein; 18g total fat; 1g fiber; 12g carbohydrates; 400mg cholesterol; 371mg sodium

Crustless Quiche

The chef at a bed-and-breakfast I recently visited on the California coast cleverly assembled crustless quiches for our breakfast—which made them perfect for gluten-free guests like me. So, I took a cue from that chef and devised this easy crustless recipe, which is also quite versatile. For a vegetarian version, replace the bacon with diced vegetables such as blanched asparagus or green beans, chopped dried tomatoes, or a handful of baby spinach.

MAKES 2 SERVINGS

¼ cup (1 ounce) shredded or finely diced Swiss cheese or cheese alternative

1 teaspoon dried minced onion

1 bacon strip, cooked and crumbled

2 large eggs

¼ cup cream or milk of choice

⅛ teaspoon (dash) granulated sugar

¹⁄₁₆ teaspoon (pinch) freshly grated nutmeg

⅛ teaspoon (dash) salt

⅛ teaspoon (dash) freshly ground black pepper

1. Preheat the oven to 375°F. Generously grease an 8-inch ovenproof skillet or pie plate. Scatter the cheese, onion, and bacon evenly over the bottom of the skillet.

2. In a small bowl, whisk together the eggs, cream, sugar, nutmeg, salt, and pepper until very smooth. Pour the egg mixture into the skillet.

3. Bake until the top is golden brown and puffy, 20 to 25 minutes. Let stand 5 minutes, and cut into slices to serve.

Per serving: 215 calories; 11g protein; 17g total fat; 1g fiber; 3g carbohydrates; 229mg cholesterol; 287mg sodium

Baked Eggs in Ham Baskets

Years ago, I had this dish at a bed-and-breakfast near Zion National Park in Utah and I was smitten with how pretty the baskets were, yet so easy. I went home and immediately crafted my own version. Depending on the size and shape of your ham slices, you may need to cut or tear them so they form a ruffled basket for the egg. If you're feeling especially hungry, simply double the ingredients to make four baskets. For a Southwest touch, skip the pesto and serve with a tablespoon of Mexican salsa on top.

MAKES 2 SERVINGS

4 very thin slices Black Forest ham (or two large slices)

1 small plum tomato or 4 cherry or grape tomatoes, seeded and finely diced

2 teaspoons store-bought pesto (optional, but adds wonderful flavor)

2 tablespoons chopped fresh chives or parsley (or 1 tablespoon dried), plus extra for garnish

2 large eggs, at room temperature

1/16 teaspoon (pinch) salt

1/16 teaspoon (pinch) freshly ground black pepper

1. Preheat the oven to 375°F. Generously grease two of the cups of a standard 6-muffin pan.

2. Gently press 2 slices of ham into each greased cup, positioning the ham so it creates a basket within each cup. Divide the diced tomatoes, pesto (if using), and chives between the cups. Break an egg into each cup and poke the yolk with a fork. Sprinkle each egg with salt and pepper.

3. Bake for 12 to 15 minutes for soft eggs, 15 to 25 minutes for hard-cooked eggs, or until the eggs reach desired doneness. The eggs continue to cook after you remove them from the oven, so don't overcook. Remove the baskets from the muffin cups and serve immediately, garnished with the chives.

STORE-BOUGHT PESTO Store-bought pesto is a great ingredient for small households. It perks up egg dishes like this, but it's also great brushed on chicken while grilling, added to salad dressings, and incorporated into breakfast casseroles such as the Sausage and Egg Strata (page 44). A jar of it keeps well in the fridge. For a dairy-free version, look for the Meditalia brand.

Per serving: 158 calories; 17g protein; 9g total fat; 1g fiber; 3g carbohydrates; 218mg cholesterol; 569mg sodium

Chilaquiles

(V)

Chilaquiles (pronounced tchee-lah-KEE-lehs) is a popular Southwest dish, originally developed by thrifty cooks to use up leftovers. Today, it's the perfect Sunday brunch or light dinner for two, served with some fresh fruit on the side. The spiciness depends on the salsa you use. Some cooks like to bake their own corn tortillas into chips in the oven, but I like the ease of store-bought chips so I just use them right out of the bag.

MAKES 2 SERVINGS

½ (15-ounce) can black or pinto beans, rinsed and drained

1 cup Mexican salsa

12 large corn tortilla chips

¼ cup (1 ounce) shredded cheddar, mozzarella, or pepper jack cheese, or cheese alternative

1 teaspoon canola oil

2 large eggs

1 ripe avocado, peeled, seeded, and diced

2 tablespoons chopped fresh cilantro

1 lime, halved (optional)

1. In a small skillet, combine the beans and salsa and cook over medium heat until heated through, about 5 minutes. Add the tortilla chips and stir to combine. Divide evenly between two large soup bowls and sprinkle each with the cheese.

2. Wipe out the skillet. Add the oil and heat over medium-high heat. Add the eggs and cook until sunny-side up, about 3 minutes (or your preferred style). Place the eggs in the bowls, top with the avocado and cilantro, and serve with a squeeze of lime, if you like.

LEFTOVER SALSA AND BEANS If you purchase a bottle of salsa for this recipe, you will have some leftover. Use it to top Baked Eggs in Ham Baskets (page 49). The leftover beans can be refrigerated and added to the Green Chile–Pork Stew (page 73), or used in the Layered Bean-Tortilla Casserole (page 132).

Per serving: 575 calories; 24g protein; 29g total fat; 16g fiber; 62g carbohydrates; 202mg cholesterol; 778mg sodium

Chia Breakfast Pudding ⓥ

Chia is a South American seed known for its extraordinary nutritional qualities. The Mayan word chia *means "stamina" or "strength," and Aztec warriors used it for endurance. It's a cinch to make this cool pudding; I often enjoy it for breakfast during the hot summer months when hot cereal just seems, well . . . too hot. The consistency is similar to tapioca pudding, with little chewy balls. If you prefer a smoother texture, grind the chia seeds in a blender before blending with the other ingredients.*

MAKES 2 SERVINGS
(½ CUP EACH)

4 tablespoons chia seeds
(white/tan or brown/
black)

1 cup milk of choice
(I like soy, almond, or
coconut milk)

2 tablespoons sweetener
of choice: maple syrup,
agave nectar, honey,
sugar

½ teaspoon pure vanilla
or almond extract

1/16 teaspoon (pinch)
ground cinnamon
or ground nutmeg
(optional)

Fresh fruit such as
strawberries, raspberries,
or blueberries, for
garnish (optional)

1. Shake all of the ingredients, except the fruit, together in a screw-top glass jar and refrigerate overnight. Or, to make single-serving jars, divide the ingredients evenly between two small Mason jars.

2. Shake or whisk the pudding a few times during the first 2 hours of chilling to redistribute the seeds or they will stick together and leave a gummy layer at the bottom of the jar.

3. Serve chilled, garnished with fresh fruit, if using.

Chocolate Chia Pudding: To make a decadent chocolate pudding, stir in 2 tablespoons of your favorite gluten-free chocolate syrup before chilling.

USING DIFFERENT MILKS The consistency of this pudding will vary depending on the type of milk you use. Nondairy milks—which vary by brand—contain different levels of stabilizers or gums, which may cause the pudding to set up more firmly. Experiment to find the right amount of chia seeds for your preferred milk.

CAN'T SHAKE IT? If you don't have the opportunity to shake the pudding during the first 2 hours, add a tablespoon of plain yogurt with the other ingredients. This will keep the chia seeds suspended in the liquid.

Per serving: 245 Calories; 9g protein; 9g total fat; 1g fiber;
34g carbohydrates; 5mg cholesterol 75mg sodium

Hearty Basic Granola ⓥ

This is a basic granola recipe with just nuts and coconut, but you can add your own dried fruits—about 1 cup total of cranberries, apricots, blueberries, cherries, or any combination—after it is baked. It is much cheaper to make your own granola than to buy it, and homemade granola is usually lower in fat and calories than store-bought versions.

MAKES 4 SERVINGS
(ABOUT ¾ CUP EACH)

2 cups gluten-free rolled oats*

½ cup coconut flakes

¼ cup sunflower seeds

¼ cup pumpkin seeds

¼ cup slivered almonds

½ teaspoon ground cinnamon

¼ teaspoon salt

2 tablespoons hot (120°F) water

¼ cup honey or maple syrup

¼ cup packed brown sugar

3 tablespoons canola oil

2 teaspoons pure vanilla extract

1. Place a rack in the middle of the oven. Preheat the oven to 350°F. Line a 9x13-inch rimmed baking sheet (not nonstick) with parchment paper.

2. In a large mixing bowl, stir together the oats, coconut, sunflower seeds, pumpkin seeds, almonds, cinnamon, and salt until thoroughly blended.

3. In a measuring cup, whisk together the hot water, honey, brown sugar, oil, and vanilla until blended. With a spatula, toss this mixture with the oat mixture until thoroughly coated, and then use the spatula to spread the granola into a thin layer on the pan.

4. Bake, stirring every 10 minutes to promote even browning, until the granola is lightly browned, 20 to 30 minutes. For darker granola, bake in additional 5-minute increments, stirring each time. Watch carefully to avoid burning. Cool the granola completely on the pan. Store in an airtight container in a dark, dry place.

Check with your physician to make sure oats are acceptable for your diet.

Per serving: 535 calories; 11g protein; 26g total fat; 8g fiber; 69g carbohydrates; 0mg cholesterol; 210mg sodium

Overnight Muesli

Hearty and creamy, muesli is a European-style breakfast food. Use this basic recipe as a starting point to tailor your own special version. For example, when I want to boost my fiber intake I often stir in a tablespoon of chia seeds, ground flaxseed meal, hemp seeds, or bran from (gluten-free) oats or rice. Use whatever you like and make this recipe your own. The sweetness comes from the grated apple and yogurt, so if you use plain, unsweetened yogurt, you might want to add a little honey, agave nectar, or maple syrup.

MAKES 2 SERVINGS

½ cup gluten-free rolled oats*

1 very small apple, grated

½ cup unsweetened yogurt of choice

½ cup milk of choice

2 tablespoons chopped nuts (walnuts, pecans, or almonds)

2 tablespoons chopped dried apricots

2 tablespoons dried cranberries

¼ teaspoon ground cinnamon

¼ teaspoon grated nutmeg (optional)

In a glass bowl with a tight-sealing lid, stir all of the ingredients until well combined. Seal tightly and refrigerate overnight. If you prefer thinner, softer muesli you can stir in more milk.

MAKE-AHEAD MUESLI Muesli will keep refrigerated for up to 3 days, so this is a great breakfast to make ahead when you have a few minutes of spare time.

Check with your physician to make sure oats are acceptable for your diet.

Per serving: 240 calories; 11g protein; 7g total fat; 5g fiber; 36g carbohydrates; 4mg cholesterol; 79mg sodium

Strawberry Green Smoothies

I am a huge fan of vegetables for breakfast, but they don't have to be visible for us to benefit from their nutrients. In this case, the veggies are hidden in a delicious smoothie. If you don't like the look of green smoothies, just use fewer greens. My philosophy is that some greens are better than no greens.

**MAKES 2 SMOOTHIES
(1 CUP EACH)**

1 cup strawberries
(or raspberries or
blueberries), preferably
frozen, but fresh is okay

1 cup milk of choice

½ cup (about a handful)
fresh spinach or kale

1 small ripe banana

¼ cup unflavored
protein powder (or
amount suggested by
manufacturer for
2 servings)

1 teaspoon honey, maple
syrup, or agave nectar
(optional)

1 or 2 ice cubes
(optional, but helpful if
the fruit isn't frozen)

Place all of the ingredients in a blender and blend until very, very smooth. Pour into glasses and serve immediately.

Per serving: 185 calories; 14g protein; 3g total fat; 3g fiber; 28g carbohydrates; 5mg cholesterol; 193mg sodium

Soups, Stews & Sandwiches

Soups and stews are versatile:

They make a great main dish or first course, or a light lunch or snack. Sometimes they are a fall-back choice when nothing else sounds good. At our house, a stormy day automatically means soup for lunch because it is warm and comforting. (In fact, warming the bowls before serving is a nice touch, too.)

But soups and stews can be perilous because the typical thickeners—wheat flour, bread crumbs—contain gluten. Choosing the right substitute thickener—and the right amount—can be confusing. In addition, soups contain many ingredients (hence, all that flavor) so downsizing in the right proportions can be hard.

With this in mind, I chose these soups and stews because they require multiple ingredients and/or a thickener. Most soups will yield 1 to 1½ cups per serving, although stews yield closer to 2 cups because they are all-in-one meals.

Some soups or stews can be cooked on the cooktop or in a slow cooker. However, when a stew calls for baking in the oven, don't cook it on the cooktop, as liquids can evaporate too quickly, leading to a dry stew. Sandwiches present their own unique challenge for people eating gluten free. In this chapter I offer recipes for those sandwiches that require multiple ingredients and that we all miss on a gluten-free diet.

Asparagus Soup

Unlike my husband, who as a child secretly axed the asparagus in his mother's garden so he wouldn't have to eat it, I eat asparagus as often as I can. Here is the ultimate springtime soup for us asparagus lovers. Serve it in coffee cups for a cute touch. You can choose which herb you want to use in the soup; each is delicious. Or, try the variations for Broccoli Soup or Cauliflower Soup below.

MAKES 2 SERVINGS
(ABOUT 1 CUP EACH)

1 (14-ounce) can (1¾ cups) gluten-free low-sodium chicken or vegetable broth, divided

¼ pound fresh asparagus, or ½ (10-ounce) package frozen

1 small leek, white parts only, thoroughly cleaned, rinsed, and diced or 2 tablespoons diced onion

1 teaspoon unsalted butter or buttery spread

¼ teaspoon salt, or to taste

⅛ teaspoon (dash) freshly ground black pepper

½ teaspoon chopped fresh herbs (dill, tarragon, thyme, or chives), plus extra for garnish

1½ teaspoons sweet rice flour or ¾ teaspoon cornstarch

1. In a medium saucepan, bring half of the broth, the asparagus, leek, butter, salt, and pepper to a boil over high heat. Reduce the heat to low and simmer, covered, for about 5 minutes, until the asparagus and leek are tender.

2. With a slotted spoon, transfer the asparagus and leek to a blender. Add the remaining broth, the herbs, and rice flour and puree for about 1 minute, until the mixture is very smooth.

3. Transfer the mixture back to the pan and cook the soup over medium heat until it is slightly thickened, 3 to 5 minutes. Serve immediately, garnished with fresh herbs.

Cream of Broccoli Soup: Replace the asparagus with the same amount of 1-inch chunks of fresh or frozen broccoli. Proceed as directed. This variation is an excellent way to use up broccoli spears that have been trimmed from the florets.

Per serving: 110 calories; 12g protein; 2g total fat; 3g fiber; 12g carbohydrates; 5mg cholesterol; 744mg sodium

Cream of Cauliflower Soup: Replace the asparagus with the same amount of 1-inch chunks of fresh cauliflower. Use 1 teaspoon grated Parmesan cheese or soy Parmesan and 1/16 teaspoon (pinch) grated nutmeg in place of the fresh herbs. Proceed as directed.

Per serving: 120 calories; 13g protein; 3g total fat; 2g fiber; 12g carbohydrates; 7mg cholesterol; 730mg sodium

Per serving: 105 calories; 12g protein; 2g total fat; 2g fiber; 12g carbohydrates; 5mg cholesterol; 730mg sodium

Creamy Tomato Soup

There are many gluten-free tomato soups on the market, but making your own from scratch—even if it's only for two people—is immensely gratifying once you taste the super-fresh flavor. I use canned whole tomatoes here, but if you have a few fresh tomatoes straight from the vine, you will be hugely rewarded. You'll need about 3 medium fresh tomatoes, peeled (see below) and chopped; you may want to increase the salt to taste. The rice helps thicken the soup.

MAKES 2 SERVINGS
(ABOUT 1 CUP EACH)

1 (14.5-ounce) can
(1¾ cups) peeled,
whole tomatoes,
including juices

¼ cup gluten-free low-
sodium chicken or
vegetable broth

2 tablespoons diced
fresh onion or
1 teaspoon dried
minced onion

2 tablespoons long-grain
white rice

1 small garlic clove
(optional)

1 teaspoon tomato paste
(see Note)

¼ teaspoon granulated
sugar

Salt and freshly ground
black pepper

2 tablespoons cream,
sour cream, or sour
cream alternative

2 teaspoons chopped
fresh basil, thyme, or
parsley, for garnish

1. Combine the tomatoes, broth, onion, rice, garlic, tomato paste, sugar, and ⅛ teaspoon (dash) salt in a 1-quart soup pot. Bring to a boil over high heat, reduce the heat to low, and simmer, covered, for 20 minutes. Stir in the cream.

2. With an immersion blender, puree the soup until it is smooth. Or, transfer the soup to a blender and puree in batches, being careful to cover the lid with a towel to avoid hot splatters. Return the soup to the pot and bring to serving temperature.

3. Add salt and pepper to taste. Serve immediately, garnished with fresh basil.

PEELING FRESH TOMATOES If you use fresh tomatoes instead of canned, you'll need to peel them, which is really very quick and simple. With a sharp paring knife, cut an "X" in the bottom of a whole tomato. Immerse it in boiling water for a few seconds until the skin starts to split, then quickly transfer it to a bowl of ice water to stop the cooking. With your fingers, slide the skins from the tomato.

USING TOMATO PASTE Once I discovered tomato paste in a tube, it became a staple in my refrigerator. Just squeeze out the small amount you need and put the tube back in the fridge. No more fussing with those 6-ounce cans and figuring out how to use up the leftover tomato paste before it spoils.

Per serving: 130 calories; 4g protein; 4g total fat; 2g fiber;
20g carbohydrates; 13mg cholesterol; 240mg sodium

Gazpacho

This cool, refreshing liquid salad is perfect for light, hot-weather meals; the recipe requires absolutely no cooking, and you can make just the right amount for a two-person meal. I use canned tomato juice that contains salt, so if you use unsalted tomato juice, be sure to add salt to taste.

MAKES 2 SERVINGS
(¾ CUP EACH)

1⅓ cups canned tomato juice (two 5.5-ounce cans), divided

2 tablespoons chopped onion

1 teaspoon coarsely chopped seeded and deveined jalapeño (or to taste)

1 small garlic clove, chopped

1 teaspoon fresh lime or lemon juice

2 tablespoons diced English cucumber, plus very thin half-slices for garnish

2 tablespoons finely chopped celery

2 tablespoons chopped fresh cilantro, divided

1. In a food processor, puree ¾ cup of the tomato juice with the onion, jalapeño, garlic, and lime juice.

2. Transfer to a medium bowl and stir in the remaining tomato juice, the cucumber, celery, and 1 tablespoon of the cilantro. Divide evenly between 2 small soup bowls or goblets and chill for at least an hour to let the flavors meld.

3. Serve chilled, garnished with a half-slice of cucumber and the remaining cilantro.

Per serving: 35 calories; 2g protein; 0g total fat; 2g fiber; 9g carbohydrates; 0mg cholesterol; 24mg sodium

Minestrone

Minestrone is an Italian vegetable soup, the perfect hearty meal in a bowl. The level of spiciness will depend on the sausage. Use the recipe as a guideline and vary the vegetables as you wish: Perhaps a handful of green beans, spinach, or Swiss chard instead of the zucchini. For a vegetarian soup, use vegetable broth, omit the sausage, and add another ⅛ teaspoon Italian seasoning.

MAKES 2 SERVINGS (2 CUPS EACH)

1 teaspoon olive oil

4 ounces gluten-free lean ground Italian sausage meat; or a 4-ounce link, cut into ⅛-inch slices

½ small onion, sliced

1 (14.5-ounce) can (1¾ cups) gluten-free low-sodium beef or vegetable broth

½ (14.5-ounce) can (¾ cup) diced tomatoes, including juice

½ (14.5-ounce) can (¾ cup) cannellini (white kidney) beans, rinsed and drained

1 medium carrot, cut into ¼-inch diagonal slices

½ small zucchini, cut into ¼-inch slices

1 small garlic clove, minced

½ teaspoon Italian seasoning

1/16 teaspoon (pinch) salt, or to taste

⅛ teaspoon (dash) freshly ground black pepper

1 small bay leaf

¼ cup gluten-free elbow macaroni

1 tablespoon grated Parmesan cheese or soy Parmesan, for garnish

1. In a heavy 3-quart saucepan with a tight-fitting lid, heat the oil over medium heat. Add the sausage and onion and cook, stirring, until the sausage is browned and the onion is soft, about 5 minutes.

2. Add the remaining ingredients except the macaroni and Parmesan. Bring to a boil, reduce the heat to low, cover, and simmer for 30 minutes.

3. Add the pasta and simmer just until the pasta is done, about 10 minutes for most brands. Remove the bay leaf and serve immediately with a dusting of Parmesan.

Per serving: 580 calories; 38g protein; 22g total fat; 15g fiber; 64g carbohydrates; 45mg cholesterol; 1019mg sodium

New England Clam Chowder

The only way I get to enjoy New England clam chowder is when I make it myself, so this recipe is "well-worn" at our house. Served with a green salad and some Cornbread (page 168), it can be Sunday night supper. Remember—the richer the milk, the creamier the soup.

MAKES 2 SERVINGS
(ABOUT 1¼ CUPS EACH)

½ slice uncooked bacon, finely chopped

1 (8-ounce) bottle clam broth

1 small russet potato (about 6 ounces), peeled and diced

¼ cup chopped celery

1 teaspoon dried minced onion

½ teaspoon chopped fresh thyme, or ⅛ teaspoon dried thyme

⅛ teaspoon (dash) garlic powder

⅛ teaspoon (dash) salt

¹⁄₁₆ teaspoon (pinch) freshly ground black pepper

1 cup whole milk or milk of choice (see note), divided

1 tablespoon potato starch or cornstarch

1 (6.5-ounce) can chopped clams with liquid

2 tablespoons chopped fresh parsley, for garnish

1. In a 2-quart saucepan, cook the bacon over medium heat until brown and crispy. Add the clam broth, potato, celery, onion, thyme, garlic powder, salt, and pepper. Bring to a boil, reduce the heat, and simmer, covered, for 15 minutes, until the potatoes are tender.

2. Add ¾ cup of the milk. Whisk the potato starch into the remaining ¼ cup milk until smooth, then add to the pan. Cook, stirring constantly, until the mixture thickens, about 3 minutes. Stir in the clams and their liquid and heat to serving temperature. Ladle into 2 bowls, garnish with parsley, and serve.

USING NONDAIRY MILKS If you use a low-protein nondairy milk such as rice milk, you may need an additional teaspoon of potato starch (or cornstarch) to thicken the soup to the desired consistency.

Per serving: 330 calories; 30g protein; 7g total fat; 1g fiber; 35g carbohydrates; 80mg cholesterol; 793mg sodium

Split Pea Soup with Bacon

This is a beloved cold-weather dish at our house. At the first sign of fall, I stock up on split peas so I can make it anytime. Sometimes I use a small ham hock (instead of the bacon) for a meatier, more flavorful soup; if you go this route, you'll need less salt. You can omit the meat altogether for a vegetarian soup.

MAKES 2 SERVINGS
(ABOUT 1¼ CUPS EACH)

½ cup split peas

1 slice uncooked bacon, chopped

2 tablespoons chopped onion

1 small carrot, peeled and cut into ¼-inch slices

1 small garlic clove, minced

1 (14.5-ounce) can (1¾ cups) gluten-free low-sodium chicken or vegetable broth

¾ cup water

⅛ teaspoon (dash) salt

1 tablespoon fresh lemon juice or sherry vinegar (optional)

1 tablespoon chopped fresh parsley, for garnish

1. Rinse the peas thoroughly.

2. In a 3-quart soup pot, cook the bacon over medium heat until crisp, about 3 minutes. Remove all but 1 tablespoon of the fat. Add the onion and carrot and cook, stirring constantly, until the vegetables start to soften, about 2 minutes. Add the peas, garlic, broth, water, and salt.

3. Bring the soup to a boil, reduce the heat to medium-low, and simmer, covered, for 35 to 40 minutes, until the peas are tender and the mixture thickens slightly. Just before serving, stir in the lemon juice, if using. Serve immediately, garnished with parsley.

FOR A CREAMIER SOUP Split peas naturally thicken as they break down during cooking, but if you prefer an even creamier, smoother soup, use an immersion blender to puree it right in the soup pot. Or remove about ½ cup and puree in a blender, then stir the pureed portion back into the pot.

SLOW-COOKER METHOD Slow cooking is my favorite way to make split pea soup. Start with a slice of cooked, chopped bacon, and use 1 tablespoon dried minced onion rather than fresh onion. Stir all of the ingredients together in a small slow cooker (2- to 4-quart) and cook for 4 to 6 hours on Low.

Per serving: 255 calories; 23g protein; 2g total fat; 14g fiber; 37g carbohydrates; 3mg cholesterol; 595mg sodium

Chicken Soup with Dumplings

Dumplings are so comforting! I enjoyed Czech and German foods while growing up in eastern Nebraska and really missed dumplings when gluten left my life. Dark chicken meat yields a more deeply flavored soup than white meat, but use what you have.

MAKES 2 SERVINGS
(1½ CUPS SOUP EACH, PLUS DUMPLINGS)

Soup

1 teaspoon canola oil

¼ cup chopped onion

2½ cups gluten-free low-sodium chicken broth

1 cup diced cooked chicken

1 small carrot, thinly sliced

2 teaspoons chopped fresh thyme or 1 teaspoon dried

1/16 teaspoon (pinch) celery salt, or to taste

1/16 teaspoon (pinch) freshly ground white pepper

1/16 teaspoon (pinch) grated nutmeg (optional)

⅓ cup frozen green peas

2 tablespoons chopped fresh parsley or 1 teaspoon dried, plus more for garnish

1 teaspoon lemon juice (optional)

Dumplings

½ cup Carol's Gluten-Free Flour Blend (page 24)

½ teaspoon baking powder

1/16 teaspoon (pinch) xanthan gum

1/16 teaspoon (pinch) salt

1 teaspoon canola oil or vegetable oil

¼ cup gluten-free low-sodium chicken broth

continued~

1. Make the soup: In a 3-quart soup pot, heat the oil over medium heat. Add the onion and cook, stirring occasionally, until translucent, about 5 minutes. Add the broth, chicken, carrot, and thyme. Bring to a boil, reduce the heat to low, and simmer, covered, for 20 minutes. Season with celery salt and pepper and add the nutmeg, if using. Depending on the saltiness of the broth, you may need more or less celery salt. Tasting is important at this stage.

2. Meanwhile, make the dumplings: In a small bowl, whisk together the flour blend, baking powder, xanthan gum, and salt until well blended. With a fork or pastry cutter, mash the oil into the mixture until it resembles pea-size crumbles. Add the broth and stir with a spatula until a stiff dough forms.

3. With the broth at a simmer, drop 8 heaping teaspoons of the dough into the broth. Cover with a tight-fitting lid and simmer on low for 5 minutes. Add the peas, parsley, and lemon juice to the soup and simmer, covered, 3 to 5 more minutes, or until the dumplings are cooked through.

4. Remove from the heat and let stand, covered, for 5 minutes. Serve, garnished with additional parsley.

Chicken Noodle Soup: You can adjust this recipe easily to make a comforting Chicken Noodle Soup. Simply omit the dumplings and cook ½ cup gluten-free spiral or penne pasta (according to package directions) in the soup.

Per serving: 540 calories; 39g protein; 22g total fat; 4g fiber; 41g carbohydrates; 85mg cholesterol; 1050mg sodium

Potato-Leek Soup

Smooth and creamy, this is a great lunch on a winter's day. But if you simply add a few slices of sausage or some chopped ham you have a hearty soup for Sunday-night supper.

MAKES 2 SERVINGS
(ABOUT 1¼ CUPS EACH)

1 (14.5-ounce) can
(1¾ cups) gluten-free
low-sodium chicken or
vegetable broth

1 medium russet potato
(about 8 ounces), peeled
and diced

1 small leek, white part
only, thoroughly cleaned,
rinsed, and thinly sliced;
or ½ cup diced onion

¼ cup thinly sliced
celery

1 teaspoon chopped
fresh thyme or
½ teaspoon dried

¼ teaspoon salt, or to
taste

1 small bay leaf

½ cup half-and-half
or milk of choice (the
richer, the better)

2 tablespoons chopped
fresh parsley, for garnish

1. In a 2-quart saucepan, bring the broth, potato, leek, celery, thyme, salt, and bay leaf to a boil. Reduce the heat to low and simmer, covered, for 15 to 20 minutes, until the potato is tender.

2. Remove the pan from the heat and remove the bay leaf. With an immersion blender, puree the soup until it is as smooth as you prefer. Or, transfer the soup to a blender in batches and puree, being careful to cover the lid with a towel to avoid hot splatters. Return the soup to the pan.

3. Add the half-and-half and heat to serving temperature over medium heat, but do not boil. Taste and add more salt, if desired. Divide the soup into 2 soup bowls and serve, garnished with parsley.

Per serving: 185 calories; 13g protein; 7g total fat; 2g fiber; 18g carbohydrates; 22mg cholesterol; 771mg sodium

 Chili

This is the first dish I ever prepared for my husband, long before we married. Why? It's probably the only dish I knew how to make (though he didn't know that at the time). I still make it. In fact, when cold weather arrives, he starts asking for it, and it has nurtured us through many a cold spell. This recipe intentionally makes two generous servings (because who doesn't love chili?) or four small servings. It also makes great leftovers.

MAKES 4 CUPS
(FOUR 1-CUP SERVINGS OR
TWO 2-CUP SERVINGS)

½ pound lean ground beef

¼ cup diced onion

1 (15-ounce) can pinto or kidney beans, rinsed and drained

1 (15-ounce) can whole tomatoes, chopped with knife or scissors

2 tablespoons diced green pepper

2 teaspoons chili powder

½ teaspoon ground cumin

½ teaspoon ground coriander

½ teaspoon salt

1 teaspoon gluten-free Worcestershire sauce

1 tablespoon chopped fresh cilantro, for garnish

Water, if needed

1. In a 3-quart saucepan, cook the ground beef and onion over medium heat, stirring, until both are gently browned and all juices are absorbed.

2. Add the remaining ingredients, except the cilantro, cover, and simmer over low heat for 2 hours. If the chili looks dry, add a bit of water as needed. Serve immediately, garnished with cilantro.

SLOW-COOKER METHOD You can also make this chili in a slow cooker. Simply cook the meat and onion as in Step 1, then add all ingredients to a 2-quart slow cooker. Cook on Low for 4 to 6 hours.

LEFTOVER CHILI This recipe makes 4 cups, which might be perfect for a meal, or might leave you with some leftovers. If you're looking for smaller portions, you can serve 2 1-cup bowls, and then use the remainder to top 2 baked potatoes at a later meal.

Per 1-cup serving: 300 calories; 19g protein; 13g total fat; 7g fiber; 29g carbohydrates; 43mg cholesterol; 832mg sodium

Hearty Beef Stew

Beef stew is comforting, and it reminds me of home. The recipe starts from scratch, but if you have cooked meat, potatoes, and vegetables on hand, the stew comes together in a snap; I often make this stew as a way to use up leftovers from a roast beef dinner. Each serving is a meal in itself and only needs a gluten-free muffin or a piece of Cornbread (page 168) to be complete.

MAKES 2 SERVINGS
(ABOUT 1½ CUPS EACH)

2 teaspoons canola oil

½ pound lean beef stew meat, cut into ½-inch cubes

Salt and freshly ground black pepper

¾ cup gluten-free low-sodium beef broth

1 (14-ounce) can whole tomatoes, undrained and chopped with scissors or a knife

2 small red potatoes, scrubbed and quartered

½ small white onion, chopped

1 cup peeled baby carrots

2 teaspoons chopped fresh thyme, or 1 teaspoon dried, or to taste

1½ teaspoons gluten-free Worcestershire sauce

¼ teaspoon granulated sugar

1 small garlic clove, minced

1 small bay leaf (optional)

2 tablespoons chopped fresh parsley

1. In a medium (3-quart) soup pot, heat the oil over medium heat. Season the stew meat with ¼ teaspoon salt and ⅛ teaspoon (dash) pepper, add to the pot, and cook until all sides are deeply browned, 3 to 5 minutes. Add the broth and tomatoes and cook, stirring constantly, to scrape all the browned bits from the bottom.

2. Add all of the remaining ingredients except the parsley; stir to combine. Bring to a boil, then reduce the heat to low and simmer, covered, for 1 hour, until the potatoes and vegetables are tender. Remove the bay leaf.

3. For a thicker stew: Just before serving transfer about ¼ cup of the cooked potatoes to a small bowl and mash them thoroughly with a fork; stir back into the stew and bring to serving temperature. Taste and add more salt and pepper, if desired. Serve hot, garnished with the parsley.

continued~

SLOW-COOKER METHOD This stew cooks up beautifully in a slow cooker. Simply brown the meat as in Step 1, and then combine the browned meat and all ingredients (except the parsley) in a 2-quart slow cooker. Cook for 6 to 8 hours on Low.

Beef and "Barley" Soup: To make a delicious gluten-free "barley" soup, replace the potatoes with ½ cup cooked sorghum, a gluten-free grain that replicates the chewiness of cooked barley.

Per serving: 490 calories; 28g protein; 29g total fat; 6g fiber; 30g carbohydrates; 85mg cholesterol; 424mg sodium

Per serving: 500 calories; 28g protein; 28g total fat; 5g fiber; 34g carbohydrates; 85mg cholesterol; 430mg sodium

Green Chile–Pork Stew

Living in the Southwest means we crave green chiles. This stew is super-easy, satisfyingly hearty, and a weekly standby dish at our house. Perfect anytime, but especially when you want an easy yet stick-to-your-ribs stew with plenty of flavor. To save time, I use cooked leftover pork tenderloin or pork chops. If you start with raw pork, allow extra time for browning. The stew is a meal in itself, but I usually serve it with homemade Cornbread (page 168) or warmed corn tortillas.

MAKES 2 SERVINGS
(1½ CUPS EACH)

1 tablespoon olive oil

½ small onion, diced

1 carrot, peeled and cut into ¼-inch slices

8 ounces cooked pork, cut into 1-inch cubes

1 (10-ounce) can mild diced tomatoes and green chiles

1 (14.5-ounce) can gluten-free low-sodium chicken broth or 1¾ cups gluten-free low-sodium chicken broth

1 cup diced peeled potato (about 4 ounces)

¼ teaspoon dried oregano

¼ teaspoon ground cumin

¼ teaspoon ground coriander

⅛ teaspoon (dash) freshly ground black pepper, or to taste

4 tablespoons chopped fresh cilantro, divided

1. In a 3-quart soup pot, heat the oil over medium heat. Add the onion and carrot and cook, stirring constantly, until slightly tender, about 3 minutes.

2. Add the remaining ingredients, using half of the cilantro. Bring the stew to a boil, reduce the heat to low, and simmer, covered, for 30 minutes.

3. For a thicker stew, just before serving, remove ¼ cup of the cooked potatoes and mash thoroughly with a fork. Then stir them back into the stew.

4. Divide the stew between 2 bowls and serve, garnished with the remaining cilantro.

Per serving: 490 calories; 44g protein; 24g total fat; 3g fiber; 26g carbohydrates; 93mg cholesterol; 1108mg sodium

 Sloppy Joes

Sloppy Joes bring back fond memories of childhood. Try my small-batch Joes, because adulthood, small households, and gluten-free diets should not prevent our continued enjoyment! Both the sweetness and the salt come from the ketchup.

MAKES 2 SANDWICHES

½ pound lean ground beef

⅓ cup ketchup

2 tablespoons water

1 teaspoon dried minced onion

1 very small garlic clove, minced; or ¹⁄₁₆ teaspoon (pinch) garlic powder

½ teaspoon gluten-free Worcestershire sauce

½ teaspoon yellow mustard

½ teaspoon cornstarch

⅛ teaspoon (dash) chili powder

⅛ teaspoon (dash) dried thyme

¹⁄₁₆ teaspoon (pinch) ground cloves or allspice (optional)

2 gluten-free hamburger buns, gently warmed

1. In a heavy 2-quart saucepan over medium-high heat, cook the ground beef until deeply browned and the moisture is evaporated, 5 to 7 minutes.

2. Add the ketchup, water, onion, garlic, Worcestershire sauce, mustard, cornstarch, chili powder, thyme, and cloves (if using) and stir to combine. Bring to a boil, reduce the heat to low, and simmer, covered, for 10 minutes to let the flavors blend. Serve immediately on buns.

Per sandwich: 475 calories; 25g protein; 26g total fat; 2g fiber; 35g carbohydrates; 85mg cholesterol; 358mg sodium

Crispy Southwestern Tacos

In the Southwest where I live, tacos are a diet staple. They are extremely versatile, so take this recipe and modify it any way you wish—anything goes when it comes to tacos. I usually make tacos when I have leftover cooked meat (such as browned ground beef or shredded pork) in the fridge or freezer, but you can use browned ground turkey or shredded chicken as well. You can also use soft white or yellow corn tortillas instead of hard taco shells; just check the label to make sure they are gluten-free, as some corn tortilla brands also include wheat.

MAKES 2 SERVINGS
(3 SMALL TACOS EACH)

¾ cup browned lean ground beef or turkey

1½ to 2 teaspoons chili powder, or to taste

Salt and freshly ground black pepper, to taste (optional)

¼ cup diced red onion

½ plum tomato, diced

¼ cup Mexican salsa

¼ cup (1 ounce) shredded cheddar or Monterey Jack cheese, or a mix

½ cup shredded iceberg lettuce or lettuce of your choice

¼ cup chopped fresh cilantro

6 crisp gluten-free corn taco shells

1. In a small skillet over medium heat, toss the browned ground beef with the chili powder and salt and pepper (if using); heat to serving temperature.

2. For each taco, layer the beef, onion, tomato, salsa, cheese, lettuce, and cilantro in a taco shell. Serve immediately.

Per serving: 505 calories; 23g protein; 32g total fat; 6g fiber; 33g carbohydrates; 79mg cholesterol; 466mg sodium

Chicken-Cilantro Salad Wraps

Despite your best intentions, there will be the occasional piece of leftover cooked chicken. This wrap is the perfect way to use it up. There are several brands of gluten-free flour tortillas or wraps on the market; my favorites are from Toufayan and Rudi's (both available in plain, spinach, and other flavors); they are quite pliable and make terrific sandwiches.

MAKES 2 WRAPS
(WITH ABOUT ½ CUP FILLING EACH)

¾ cup finely diced cooked chicken
(about 4 ounces or 1 small chicken
breast half)

3 tablespoons light mayonnaise or
Miracle Whip salad dressing spread

2 tablespoons finely diced celery

2 tablespoons chopped fresh
cilantro

1 tablespoon sweet pickle relish

1 tablespoon chopped shallot or
green onion

1 tablespoon slivered almonds

⅛ teaspoon (dash) celery salt, or to
taste

1 tablespoon dried cranberries
(optional)

Salt and freshly ground black
pepper

2 gluten-free flour tortillas

2 small lettuce leaves

1. In a medium bowl, stir together the chicken, mayonnaise, celery, cilantro, pickle relish, shallot, almonds, celery salt, and cranberries (if using) until blended. Or for more shredded consistency, whirl the ingredients in a food processor until well blended. Taste and add salt and pepper, if desired.

2. Soften the tortillas (see below). Spread half of the chicken salad down the middle of a tortilla. Top with a lettuce leaf. Gently roll one side of the tortilla toward the center and finish rolling into a loose roll to create a wrap. Place seam side down on a serving plate, using a toothpick to keep the wrap rolled, if necessary. Repeat with the remaining tortilla, and serve immediately while the tortillas remain pliable.

SOFTENING GLUTEN-FREE FLOUR TORTILLAS
Make them pliable by steaming on a splatter guard (a flat, handled screen that keeps bacon from splattering while frying). Set the guard over a skillet of simmering water, place one tortilla on top, and steam for 5 to 10 seconds. The tortilla will soften quickly; remove it from the heat before it gets soggy. Place the steamed tortillas between sheets of parchment paper so they stay warm and soft while steaming the remaining tortillas.

Per wrap: 565 calories; 23g protein; 31g total fat; 3g fiber;
48g carbohydrates; 71mg cholesterol; 716mg sodium

Main Dishes

When people think of preparing

a meal for two, it is usually the main dish or entrée that first comes to mind. But the typical entrée recipe serves four or six people, leaving a mish-mash of leftovers for your small household to deal with. Over a week's time, those leftovers pile up and may go to waste—or you eat the same thing day after day after day. How boring!

For our main dishes, I've chosen old favorites, all-American dishes, and an array of ethnic specialties (Mexican, Italian, Asian, French, and Mediterranean) that range from mild to spicy. A little something for everybody!

As with the stews in the previous chapter, when a dish requires cooking in the oven (such as Beef Burgundy), be sure to cook it as specified. Don't be tempted to use the cooktop or the liquids may evaporate too much, leading to a dry dish.

Preparation time: 5 minutes
Marinating time: 12 hours or overnight
Grilling time: 10 minutes

Marinated Flank Steak

You can grill this flavorful steak on the outdoor barbecue or an indoor grill pan. It serves four, so serve half of the meat one night, then use the leftovers a day or two later in sandwiches and tacos, or toss in salads for a flavorful way to easily add protein. I usually have one of these flank steaks marinating in my freezer. Defrost it in the fridge overnight and it grills in just minutes.

MAKES 4 SERVINGS
(1 POUND)

2 tablespoons gluten-free tamari soy sauce

2 tablespoons canola oil

2 tablespoons red wine vinegar

1 tablespoon gluten-free Worcestershire sauce

1 tablespoon Dijon mustard

1 small garlic clove, minced

¼ teaspoon freshly ground black pepper

1 pound flank steak (or skirt or hanger steak)

1. In a glass container with a lid or a heavy-duty resealable plastic storage bag, whisk together the tamari, oil, vinegar, Worcestershire sauce, mustard, garlic, and black pepper until well blended. Add the steak, seal tightly, and marinate (with the steak lying flat so it is immersed in the marinade) for at least 12 hours or up to overnight. (You can also freeze the steak at this point for a later meal. Use within 1 month, and defrost overnight in the fridge before grilling.)

2. When ready to cook the steak, heat an outdoor grill or indoor grill pan to medium. Remove the steak from the marinade, discard the marinade, and pat the steak dry with paper towels.

3. Grill the steak to desired doneness, or about 6 minutes per side for medium-rare, depending on the thickness of the steak. Remove the steak from the heat, let stand (tightly wrapped to keep it warm) for 5 minutes. Then slice it against the grain with a very sharp or serrated knife. Serve immediately.

Herbed Marinated Steak: In the summer, I add lots of chopped fresh herbs to the marinade—such as rosemary or thyme. You can also add dried herbs—the marinade is very flexible.

Per 4-ounce serving: 270 calories; 23g protein; 19g total fat; 1g fiber; 2g carbohydrates; 58mg cholesterol; 463mg sodium

 # Meat Loaf

This small meat loaf—one of America's favorite dishes—is perfect for two hearty servings. Or save a thin slice for a meat loaf sandwich tomorrow. Be sure to use the cloves (or allspice); it adds that special "something" that makes this meat loaf unforgettable.

MAKES 2 SERVINGS
(ONE 3¼x5¾-INCH LOAF;
CUT IN 4 SLICES)

⅓ cup low-sodium ketchup

1 small garlic clove, minced, or ¼ teaspoon garlic powder

¼ teaspoon chili powder

¹⁄₁₆ teaspoon (pinch) ground cloves or allspice

½ teaspoon gluten-free Worcestershire sauce

8 ounces lean ground beef

1 large egg, beaten

½ cup gluten-free bread crumbs (to make your own, see page 127)

2 teaspoons dried minced onion

¼ teaspoon salt

⅛ teaspoon (dash) freshly ground black pepper

1. Preheat the oven to 350°F. Generously grease a 3¼x5¾-inch nonstick loaf pan (gray, not black).

2. In a medium bowl, whisk together the ketchup, garlic, chili powder, cloves, and Worcestershire sauce until thoroughly blended. Transfer 2 tablespoons of the mixture to a small bowl and set aside.

3. To the medium bowl, add the ground beef, egg, bread crumbs, dried onion, salt, and pepper. Mix well with your hands until well blended. (Or, put all the ingredients in a quart-size plastic bag and massage with your hands from the outside.)

4. Gently pat the meat into the loaf pan. Make an indentation down the center and spread the reserved ketchup mixture on top.

5. Bake until the top is nicely browned and pulls away from the edge of the pan, and an instant-read thermometer registers 160°F when inserted into the center, 30 to 35 minutes. Let stand, covered, for 10 minutes. Cut into 4 slices and serve.

CRUSTIER MEAT LOAF If you like a crustier loaf, shape the meat mixture into 2 individual loaves on a sheet pan and bake until browned and crusty on top, 20 to 25 minutes.

Per serving: 490 calories; 28g protein; 28g total fat; 2g fiber; 32g carbohydrates; 178mg cholesterol; 630mg sodium

Orange Beef Stir-Fry

Stir-fried dishes are perfect for small households because you can easily vary the amount of ingredients. Once everything is prepped, the stir-fry comes together very quickly, so have the rest of the meal ready when you start it. Have extra tamari nearby if you like a saltier dish.

MAKES 2 SERVINGS

Orange Sauce

⅔ cup fresh orange juice, divided

2 teaspoons cornstarch

1 tablespoon gluten-free tamari soy sauce, plus extra for sprinkling

1 teaspoon rice vinegar

1 teaspoon sesame oil or canola oil

½ teaspoon molasses (not blackstrap)

½ teaspoon sugar

1 tablespoon grated orange zest

1 small garlic clove, minced

⅛ teaspoon (dash) crushed red pepper flakes

Beef and Vegetables

1 teaspoon canola oil

8 ounces beef stew meat, cut into ½-inch cubes

½ cup ⅛-inch sliced red and/or yellow bell pepper

½ cup fresh snow peas, halved diagonally

½ cup ½-inch diagonally sliced carrots (or use baby carrots)

1½ cups hot cooked brown or white rice

2 tablespoons chopped fresh cilantro

1. Make the sauce: Pour ¼ cup of the orange juice into a small bowl and whisk in the cornstarch until smooth. Whisk in the remaining orange juice and the remaining sauce ingredients until well blended.

2. Prepare the beef and vegetables: In a medium skillet, heat the canola oil over medium-high heat. Add the beef and cook, stirring occasionally, until browned on all sides, 2 to 3 minutes. Reduce the heat to medium and add the bell pepper, snow peas, and carrots and cook for 1 minute, stirring constantly.

3. Stir in the sauce and simmer until it thickens slightly and the vegetables are crisp-tender, 1 to 2 minutes. Sprinkle with additional tamari, if desired. Serve over hot cooked rice, garnished with cilantro.

Per serving: 490 calories; 29g protein; 16g total fat; 5g fiber; 57g carbohydrates; 62mg cholesterol; 383mg sodium

Hungarian Beef Goulash

Hungary's version of beef stew uses Hungarian paprika, caraway seeds, and sour cream for its distinct flavor. I serve it on pasta, but some people like it with dumplings (see page 66) or boiled potatoes. We ate it with white rice when I was in Hungary. It can also be served alone. Look for Hungarian sweet paprika in kitchen stores or online.

MAKES 2 SERVINGS (1 CUP EACH)

1 teaspoon canola oil

½ pound beef stew meat, cut into ½-inch cubes

¼ teaspoon salt

⅛ teaspoon (dash) freshly ground black pepper

¾ cup ⅛-inch sliced and peeled carrots

¾ cup diced onion

1 (8-ounce) can tomato sauce

½ cup gluten-free low-sodium beef broth

1 tablespoon tomato paste

1 small garlic clove, chopped

1 teaspoon apple cider vinegar

1 tablespoon Hungarian sweet paprika

1/16 teaspoon (pinch) caraway seed

1 small bay leaf

2 tablespoons sour cream or sour cream alternative

6 ounces gluten-free pasta (egg noodles, penne, rotini), cooked

1 tablespoon chopped fresh parsley, for garnish

1. Place a rack in the middle of the oven. Preheat the oven to 325°F.

2. In a heavy, 2-quart lidded saucepan, heat the canola oil over medium heat. Add the beef, sprinkle with salt and pepper, and cook until browned on all sides, about 5 minutes. With a slotted spoon, transfer the beef to a plate. Add the carrots and onion to the pan and cook over medium heat, stirring constantly, until the vegetables start to brown, about 5 minutes.

3. Return the meat to the pan and stir in the tomato sauce, broth, tomato paste, garlic, vinegar, paprika, caraway seed, and bay leaf. Bring to a boil, stirring constantly to capture any browned bits from the pan bottom.

4. Cover the pan, transfer to the oven, and bake for 1 hour. (Don't be tempted to simmer it on the cooktop because it will become too dry.)

5. Carefully remove the pan from the oven and discard the bay leaf. Pour ¼ cup of the hot stew liquid into a small bowl, and stir in the sour cream until smooth. Stir the sour cream mixture back into the stew. Taste and add salt and pepper, if desired. Serve in bowls with the noodles, garnished with parsley.

Per serving: 435 calories; 34g protein; 13g total fat; 6g fiber; 46g carbohydrates; 64mg cholesterol; 1118mg sodium

Beef Stroganoff

I didn't try stroganoff until I was in college. But once I had, I was hooked for a lifetime. There is something about the deeply flavorful creamy sauce—along with the hearty beef, mushrooms, and onions—that is very enticing. I like it served over pasta, but it is equally good with rice.

MAKES 2 SERVINGS (1 CUP EACH)

8 ounces beef stew meat, cut into ½-inch cubes

⅛ teaspoon (dash) salt, plus additional for finishing, if desired

⅛ teaspoon (dash) freshly ground black pepper, plus additional for finishing, if desired

1 tablespoon canola oil

½ cup sliced white mushrooms, such as cremini or button

¼ cup diced onion

1 small garlic clove, minced

¾ cup gluten-free low-sodium beef broth, divided

1 tablespoon tomato paste

1 tablespoon Dijon mustard

1 teaspoon chopped fresh dill, or ½ teaspoon dried dill weed

2 teaspoons sweet rice flour, or 1 teaspoon cornstarch

2 tablespoons sour cream or sour cream alternative

4 ounces gluten-free noodles, cooked; or 1½ cups cooked rice

1 tablespoon chopped fresh parsley, for garnish

⅛ teaspoon (dash) paprika, for garnish

1. Sprinkle the beef with the salt and pepper. In a heavy-lidded 3-quart saucepan, heat the oil over medium heat. Working in batches if necessary, add the beef and cook until browned on all sides and cooked through, 5 to 6 minutes. With a slotted spoon, transfer the beef to a plate. Add the mushrooms and onion to the pot and cook until the juices have evaporated, 2 to 3 minutes.

2. Add the garlic and ⅔ cup of the beef broth and cook, scraping the drippings from the bottom of the skillet. Stir in the tomato paste, mustard, and dill. Return the beef to the pan and simmer on low, covered, for 30 minutes.

3. Whisk the sweet rice flour into the remaining beef broth until smooth, then add to the pan. Increase the heat to medium and cook, stirring constantly, until the mixture thickens. Reduce the heat to low and stir in the sour cream.

4. Bring to serving temperature, but do not boil or the sour cream may curdle. Taste and add additional salt and pepper, if desired. Serve over hot cooked noodles or rice, garnished with chopped parsley and paprika.

Per serving: 500 calories; 26g protein; 21g total fat; 3g fiber; 50g carbohydrates; 50mg cholesterol; 357mg sodium

Beef Burgundy

I usually make this dish when I have leftover dry red wine. We especially enjoy it in winter, when slow-cooked dishes seem so appropriate. It can be served alone, over pasta or rice, or over Easy Microwave Polenta (page 141). A crisp tossed salad and gluten-free French Baguette (page 172) make it a perfect meal.

MAKES 2 SERVINGS (1 CUP EACH)

1 slice uncooked bacon

½ pound beef chuck stew meat, cut into ½-inch cubes

1 tablespoon cornstarch

¼ teaspoon salt, plus more to taste

¼ teaspoon freshly ground pepper, plus more to taste

½ cup cleaned and sliced white mushrooms (such as cremini or button)

¾ cup gluten-free low-sodium beef broth

½ cup Burgundy or other dry red wine

½ cup baby carrots (the smaller, the better), about 1 snack package

½ cup diced onion (or frozen pearl onions)

1 tablespoon tomato paste

1 teaspoon gluten-free Worcestershire sauce

1 small garlic clove, minced

1 tablespoon chopped fresh thyme, or ½ teaspoon dried, divided

1 bay leaf

1. Preheat the oven to 325°F. In a heavy 2-quart saucepan with a lid, cook the bacon over medium heat until crisp, 3 to 4 minutes. Remove the bacon with tongs, leaving any bacon fat in the pan.

2. Sprinkle the beef with the cornstarch. Working in batches if necessary, add the beef to the pot in a single layer (to facilitate browning). Sprinkle with the salt and pepper and cook, stirring occasionally, until the beef is thoroughly browned on all sides and cooked through, 5 to 6 minutes. Transfer to a plate.

3. Add the mushrooms to the pan and cook, stirring occasionally, until lightly browned and their juices have evaporated, 2 to 3 minutes. Crumble the cooked bacon into the pan, and stir in the browned beef, the broth, wine, carrots, onion, tomato paste, Worcestershire sauce, garlic, half of the thyme, and the bay leaf.

4. Cover and cook over low heat for 1 hour. Discard the bay leaf. Taste and add more salt and pepper, if desired. Serve in bowls (or over rice, pasta, or polenta), garnished with the remaining thyme.

Per serving: 375 calories; 22g protein; 20g total fat; 3g fiber; 17g carbohydrates; 68mg cholesterol; 494mg sodium

Stuffed Bell Peppers

This is homestyle cooking, just for two, and a meal in itself: meat, starch, and vegetable all in one gorgeous package. And it's an especially good way to use up leftover cooked rice. In fact, I often cook extra brown rice (more nutritious than white rice) to use later in the week for these peppers. For a vegetarian dish, omit the sausage and increase the Italian seasoning to ½ teaspoon.

MAKES 2 SERVINGS
(2 HALVES EACH)

2 medium red or yellow bell peppers

1 cup cooked brown or white rice

4 ounces gluten-free sweet Italian sausage (1 link), browned, drained, and finely chopped or crumbled

1 cup canned diced tomatoes

1 small garlic clove, minced

¼ teaspoon dried Italian seasoning

¼ teaspoon salt

1/16 teaspoon (pinch) crushed red pepper flakes (optional)

1/8 teaspoon (dash) freshly ground black pepper

¼ cup (1 ounce) shredded low-fat mozzarella cheese or cheese alternative

2 tablespoons chopped fresh basil or parsley

1. Place a rack in the middle of the oven. Preheat the oven to 350°F. Coat a 9-inch square microwave- and oven-safe baking dish with cooking spray.

2. Halve each pepper lengthwise, from stem to base, leaving the stems on for a prettier presentation but removing the vein and seeds. Place the pepper halves in the baking dish, cut sides up. Cover with waxed paper and cook in the microwave on High for 5 minutes to soften. Remove the dish from the microwave and let the peppers cool while making the filling.

3. In a large bowl, stir together the rice, sausage, tomatoes, garlic, Italian seasoning, salt, red pepper flakes, and black pepper. Stuff each pepper half with ½ cup of the filling, mounding it to fit if necessary.

4. Cover the dish with foil and bake until the filling is heated through, about 20 minutes. Remove the foil, sprinkle the peppers with cheese, and bake until the peppers are heated through and the cheese is melted, about 10 minutes. Remove from the oven and serve, garnished with the basil.

Per serving: 405 calories; 15g protein; 23g total fat; 5g fiber; 36g carbohydrates; 56mg cholesterol; 752mg sodium

Sausage, Bell Peppers, and Mushrooms on Pasta

I like the dish with penne pasta, but it is equally good all by itself, or spooned on Easy Microwave Polenta (page 141) or rice. A crisp salad is all you need for a complete meal.

MAKES 2 SERVINGS

1 tablespoon olive oil

4 ounces gluten-free sweet Italian sausage (1 link), cut in ⅛-inch slices

½ red bell pepper, cut vertically in ⅛-inch slices

¼ onion, cut vertically in ⅛-inch slices

1 cup sliced fresh mushrooms (or a 7.3-ounce jar, drained)

⅛ teaspoon (dash) salt, or to taste

1 large garlic clove, minced

1 teaspoon chopped fresh rosemary, or to taste

½ cup dry red wine

½ cup gluten-free low-sodium beef broth

½ teaspoon cornstarch stirred into 2 tablespoons water until smooth (optional)

4 ounces (1 cup) uncooked gluten-free penne pasta

2 tablespoons grated Parmesan cheese or soy Parmesan

1 tablespoon chopped fresh parsley, for garnish

1. In a heavy, medium saucepan with a lid, heat the oil over medium heat. Add the sausage slices and brown on both sides. Remove the sausage to a plate and discard all but 1 tablespoon of the fat remaining in the pan. Add the bell pepper, onion, mushrooms, and salt to the pan and cook, stirring constantly, until the vegetables are tender and the mushrooms have released all their juices, about 2 minutes.

2. Add the garlic, rosemary, and wine and bring to a boil. Reduce the heat to low and simmer for 1 minute to slightly reduce the wine. Add the broth and return the sausage to the pan. Simmer, covered, for 30 minutes. For a thicker sauce, stir the cornstarch-water mixture into the pan and cook until the sauce thickens slightly. Taste and add more salt, if desired.

3. Meanwhile, cook the pasta in boiling, salted water according to package directions. Drain thoroughly and divide between 2 bowls. Top with the mushroom mixture, dust with Parmesan, and sprinkle with parsley.

Per serving: 565 calories; 21g protein; 26g total fat; 3g fiber; 50g carbohydrates; 47mg cholesterol; 626mg sodium

Slow-Cooker Southwestern Pork Tenderloin

Pork tenderloin is a long, round cylinder weighing approximately 1 pound, which is perfect for halving. So, cook half (½ pound) and freeze the remaining half for another meal. It is best to use a small slow cooker—no larger than 4 quarts.

MAKES 2 SERVINGS

½ cup orange juice

1 tablespoon red wine vinegar

¼ cup diced onion

1 large garlic clove, minced

½ teaspoon ground oregano

¼ teaspoon ground cumin

⅛ teaspoon (dash) chipotle chile powder, or more to taste

1 tablespoon canola oil

½ pound pork tenderloin, trimmed of fat

½ teaspoon salt

¼ teaspoon freshly ground black pepper

1. In a small measuring cup, whisk together the orange juice, vinegar, onion, garlic, oregano, cumin, and chile powder and have it ready by your cooktop to deglaze the skillet.

2. Heat the oil in a heavy, medium skillet over medium-high heat. Pat the pork dry with paper towels and season with the salt and pepper. Brown the pork on all sides in the skillet, about 8 minutes. Transfer the pork to the slow cooker. Add the orange juice mixture to the skillet and bring to a boil, scraping the skillet with a spatula to loosen the browned bits. Pour this mixture around the pork in the slow cooker.

3. Cook 6 to 8 hours on Low heat. Remove the pork from the slow cooker, cover, and let rest for 10 minutes. Slice into medallions and serve, drizzled with a little bit of the juices from the cooker.

Leftover Tenderloin: If you have any leftover pork from this meal, use it in the Green Chile–Pork Stew (page 73).

Shredded Pulled Pork: Instead of slicing the pork, when you remove it from the cooker, shred and return to the cooker and allow the juices to moisten the meat. Use this delicious shredded meat in tacos, or serve over hot cooked brown rice, with a drizzle of the juices and a garnish of fresh chopped cilantro.

Per serving: 175 calories; 25g protein; 4g total fat; 1g fiber;
10g carbohydrates; 74mg cholesterol; 593mg sodium

Smothered Pork Chops

Homey and satisfying, these chops rest in creamy gravy surrounded by lots of flavorful onions. I like them with mashed potatoes so the gravy smothers them, too. Where I'm from in Nebraska, Lawry's seasoned salt is the norm, but I prefer the more flavorful Cajun or Creole seasoning blends instead—½ teaspoon for mild flavor and 1 teaspoon for bolder flavor. If your seasoning is heavily salted and you use a full teaspoon, you might not need all of the ¼ teaspoon salt.

MAKES 2 SERVINGS

½ to 1 teaspoon Cajun or Creole seasoning, to taste

¼ teaspoon salt

¼ teaspoon freshly ground black pepper

2 bone-in pork chops (6 ounces each, about ½ inch thick)

2 tablespoons canola oil

1 medium onion, very thinly sliced

¾ cup gluten-free low-sodium chicken broth

1 tablespoon sweet rice flour, or 1½ teaspoons cornstarch

¼ cup milk of choice (the richer the milk, the creamier the gravy)

1 tablespoon chopped fresh parsley, for garnish

1. Whisk together the seasoning, salt, and pepper, and sprinkle evenly on both of sides of the pork chops.

2. In a 9- or 10-inch heavy nonstick skillet, heat the oil over medium heat. Add the pork chops and cook until browned on one side, about 3 minutes. Turn and brown the other side, about 3 more minutes. Transfer the chops to a plate.

3. Add the onion to the skillet, cover, and cook over medium-low heat, stirring frequently, for 15 minutes, until the onion is browned and tender. (If it sticks or burns, add some water.)

4. Add the broth to the skillet. Whisk the sweet rice flour into the milk until smooth, and then whisk the milk into the skillet and continue cooking over low heat until the gravy thickens slightly. Nestle the pork chops in the gravy; cover and simmer over low heat for 8 to 10 minutes, until the pork chops are cooked through. Taste and add more seasoning, if desired. Serve immediately, garnished with a sprinkle of parsley.

Per serving: 415 calories; 28g protein; 29g total fat; 1g fiber; 10g carbohydrates; 68mg cholesterol; 578mg sodium

Sweet-and-Sour Pork

This dish is prettiest with a mix of red, yellow, and green bell peppers, but use what you have. As with all stir-fries, assembling the ingredients takes a little time—but once prepped, the meal cooks quite quickly.

MAKES 2 SERVINGS

3 teaspoons cornstarch, divided

3 teaspoons low-sodium gluten-free tamari soy sauce, divided

½ pound pork (tenderloin, chops, or shoulder), cut into ½-inch cubes

2 tablespoons cider vinegar

2 tablespoons sugar

1 tablespoon ketchup

1 (8-ounce) can pineapple chunks, drained, ¼ cup juice reserved

1 tablespoon canola oil

¼ small onion, cut into ⅛-inch slices

2 medium bell peppers, (about 1 cup), cut in ½-inch pieces

1½ teaspoons minced fresh ginger

1½ cups hot cooked brown or white rice

1. In a medium bowl, whisk together 2 teaspoons of the cornstarch and 1½ teaspoons of the tamari. Add the pork cubes and toss until thoroughly coated. In a small bowl, whisk together the remaining 1 teaspoon cornstarch and 1½ teaspoons tamari until smooth, and then whisk in the vinegar, sugar, ketchup, and pineapple juice until smooth to create a sauce.

2. In a medium skillet, heat the oil over medium heat. Add the pork cubes and cook, turning once, until browned, about 3 minutes. Add the onion and cook, stirring constantly, for 1 minute. Add the pineapple chunks, bell peppers, and ginger and cook, stirring constantly, until the peppers are slightly tender, about 3 minutes.

3. Stir in the sauce, bring to a boil, and cook, stirring constantly, until the sauce thickens, about 1 minute. Serve over hot cooked rice.

Per serving: 500 calories; 29g protein; 12g total fat; 5g fiber; 70g carbohydrates; 74mg cholesterol; 451mg sodium

Personal Pepperoni Pizza

I know this book is about cooking for two people, but what if you're the only one who wants pizza? The dough makes enough for one 8-inch pizza for one person (or two, if you feel like sharing!). The sauce makes enough for four pizzas; use ¼ cup for this pizza and freeze the rest in ¼-cup portions for three future pizzas. Or, use your favorite store-bought pizza sauce. For full-size pizza recipes, see any of my other cookbooks or my website at www.CarolFenster.com.

MAKES 1 SERVING (ONE 8-INCH PIZZA)

Pizza Sauce

1 (8-ounce) can tomato sauce

1 teaspoon sugar

1½ teaspoons Italian seasoning

½ teaspoon fennel seeds (optional)

¼ teaspoon garlic powder

¼ teaspoon salt

Dough

1½ teaspoons active dry yeast

½ teaspoon sugar

⅓ cup warm milk of choice

½ cup Carol's Gluten-Free Flour Blend (page 24)

½ teaspoon xanthan gum

½ teaspoon Italian seasoning

1 teaspoon olive oil, plus extra for brushing on crust

½ teaspoon cider vinegar

Brown rice flour, for sprinkling

Toppings

¼ cup mini pepperoni slices (or regular-size pepperoni)

⅓ cup (1.3 ounces) shredded mozzarella cheese (or more to your taste)

1. Place racks in the bottom and middle positions of the oven. Preheat the oven to 375°F. Grease an 8-inch circle on a 12-inch nonstick pizza pan (gray, not black) or a 9x13-inch nonstick baking sheet (gray, not black).

2. Make the sauce: In a small, heavy saucepan, combine all of the sauce ingredients and simmer over low heat, uncovered and stirring occasionally, for 15 minutes. Set aside.

3. Make the dough: While the sauce simmers, dissolve the yeast and sugar in the warm milk for 5 minutes. In a medium bowl, beat the warm milk mixture and the remaining dough ingredients together with an electric mixer on low speed until well blended, about 20 seconds. The dough will be very soft.

4. Place the pizza dough on the greased circle of the pan. Liberally sprinkle the dough with brown rice flour, and then press into an 8-inch circle with your hands. Continue to dust with flour to prevent sticking. Make the edges thicker to contain the toppings, taking care to make the dough as smooth and even as possible for the prettiest crust.

continued~

5. Bake the pizza crust for 10 minutes on the bottom rack of the oven. Brush the edges of the crust with a little olive oil. Spread ¼ cup pizza sauce on top. Arrange the pepperoni on the sauce and sprinkle with the cheese. Return the pizza to the middle rack and bake until nicely browned, about 10 minutes. Remove the pizza from the oven. For a shinier crust, brush the crust lightly with olive oil. Cool the pizza on a wire rack for 5 minutes, then serve hot.

MEASURING PERFECT PIZZA Use a plastic ruler to measure the diameter of your pizza. Sometimes it is hard to estimate the circle of dough, but size is important. If the circle of dough is larger than 8 inches, the crust might burn because the dough is thinner. If it is smaller than 8 inches, it may take longer to bake since the dough is thicker.

Per pizza: 810 calories; 28g protein; 42g total fat; 5g fiber; 76g carbohydrates; 84mg cholesterol; 1930mg sodium

Scalloped Potatoes with Ham

*A family favorite at our house, you will love this homey comfort-food dish.
It bakes in a thin layer in an 8-inch baking dish. You can also serve it as a
vegetarian side dish, perhaps with ½ cup of sliced mushrooms instead of ham.*

MAKES 2 SERVINGS
(ONE 8-INCH CASSEROLE)

1 large russet potato
(about 12 ounces),
peeled, quartered, and
cut into ⅛-inch slices

2 slices Canadian bacon,
about ⅛ inch thick

1 tablespoon dried
minced onion

½ teaspoon salt, divided

⅛ teaspoon (dash)
freshly ground black
pepper

1 tablespoon potato
starch or sweet rice flour

¼ teaspoon dry mustard

1⁄16 teaspoon (pinch)
grated nutmeg

1 cup milk of choice

2 teaspoons canola oil

2 tablespoons grated
Parmesan cheese or soy
Parmesan, divided

1⁄16 teaspoon (pinch)
paprika

1. Preheat the oven to 350°F. Generously grease an 8-inch baking dish with 2-inch sides.

2. In a medium bowl, toss the potato and ham with the onion, ¼ teaspoon of the salt, and the pepper. Arrange in the baking dish. In a jar with a screw-top lid, shake together the remaining ¼ teaspoon salt, the potato starch, dry mustard, and nutmeg until blended; add the milk, oil, and 1 tablespoon of the Parmesan. Shake thoroughly until the ingredients are blended to make the sauce. (Alternatively, blend the ingredients—through Parmesan—in a blender until smooth.)

3. Pour the sauce evenly over the potatoes and sprinkle the remaining 1 tablespoon Parmesan and the paprika on top. Cover with aluminum foil and bake for 50 minutes. Uncover and bake until bubbly and the potatoes are lightly browned on top, about 10 minutes more. Serve hot.

Per serving: 220 calories; 13g protein; 9g total fat; 1g fiber;
20g carbohydrates; 23mg cholesterol; 1090mg sodium

Spaghetti Pie

Simple, yet so comforting. This dish is perfect for using up leftover spaghetti (which is a shame to waste) and a stash of browned sausage in the freezer, but it is also easy to assemble from scratch as I do here. I use a 7-inch glass pie pan, but an 8-inch pan also works.

MAKES 2 SERVINGS

4 ounces gluten-free spaghetti (see Measuring Spaghetti, below)

1 large egg

1 tablespoon olive oil

2 tablespoons grated Parmesan cheese or soy Parmesan

½ cup light sour cream or sour cream alternative

4 ounces gluten-free Italian sausage meat

¾ cup store-bought gluten-free marinara or homemade Spaghetti Sauce (page 99)

¼ cup (1 ounce) shredded mozzarella cheese or cheese alternative

1. Place a rack in the middle of the oven. Preheat the oven to 350°F. Generously grease a 7- or 8-inch glass pie pan.

2. Cook the spaghetti in boiling, salted water according to package directions until cooked through but still firm to the bite. Drain and return to the pot. Meanwhile, whisk together the egg and olive oil in a small bowl, and then whisk in the Parmesan until thoroughly blended. Toss this mixture with the still-warm spaghetti until it is thoroughly coated. Press the spaghetti on the bottom and up the sides of the pie pan to form a crust. Spread the sour cream in the middle of the spaghetti, but not on the crust edges.

3. Meanwhile, in a medium skillet, cook the sausage over medium heat until browned, 3 to 4 minutes; drain any fat. Pour the spaghetti sauce into the skillet and stir until well blended.

4. Spoon the sausage mixture on top of the sour cream in the spaghetti crust; the sauce should cover the sour cream. Bake for 15 minutes. Sprinkle the mozzarella on top and bake until the cheese is melted and slightly browned, about 5 minutes.

MEASURING SPAGHETTI Two ounces is the typical recommended serving of uncooked spaghetti. So, for two people how much is 4 ounces of uncooked spaghetti? It's one-fourth of a typical 16-ounce package.

Per serving: 595 calories; 25g protein; 34g total fat; 3g fiber; 48g carbohydrates; 158mg cholesterol; 738mg sodium

Preparation time: 10 minutes
Cooking time (sauce): 2 hours (or 4 to 6 hours in a slow cooker)
Baking time (meatballs): 20 minutes

Spaghetti and Meatballs

This sauce is enough for two meals, so either refrigerate or freeze the leftovers for a second meal . . . such as Lasagna (page 100) or Spaghetti Pie (page 98).

MAKES 2 SERVINGS
(PLUS LEFTOVER SAUCE)

Spaghetti Sauce
1 (28-ounce) can whole tomatoes or 3½ cups tomato juice

1 (6-ounce) can tomato paste

2 tablespoons grated Romano or Parmesan cheese (optional)

1½ tablespoons dried parsley

1 tablespoon dried basil

1½ teaspoons dried rosemary, crushed

1 teaspoon dried oregano

½ teaspoon sugar

½ teaspoon salt

¼ teaspoon crushed red pepper

Meatballs
½ pound lean ground beef

¼ cup gluten-free bread crumbs (to make your own, see page 127)

1 large egg

1 teaspoon Italian seasoning

¼ teaspoon salt

¼ teaspoon freshly ground black pepper

6 ounces gluten-free spaghetti or fettuccine (see Measuring Spaghetti, page 98)

1. Make the sauce: In a medium saucepan, combine all of the sauce ingredients and simmer over low heat for 2 hours. Or, use a 2-quart slow cooker and cook for 4 to 6 hours on Low. (Makes 4 cups.)

2. Preheat the oven to 350°F. Line a 9x13-inch rimmed baking sheet with foil or parchment paper.

3. Make the meatballs: In a medium bowl, combine all of the meatball ingredients and mix together with a spatula or your hands until blended. Shape into eight 1½-inch balls and place on the baking sheet. Bake until cooked through, about 20 minutes. Keep warm or refrigerate for up to 1 day; reheat the meatballs in the microwave oven or add to the sauce and reheat in a saucepan at serving time.

4. To serve, cook the spaghetti in boiling, salted water according to package directions until cooked through but still firm to the bite. Drain and transfer to a serving bowl. Top with 2 cups of the sauce and all the meatballs and serve.

FOR A SMOOTHER SAUCE Puree the tomatoes in a blender, chop them with kitchen scissors, or use tomato juice instead of whole tomatoes if you'd like a smoother sauce.

Per serving: 785 calories; 40g protein; 28g total fat; 8g fiber; 92g carbohydrates; 181mg cholesterol; 1168mg sodium

 Lasagna

Using sweet Italian sausage makes this lasagna more flavorful, but plain ground beef works just fine. It's easiest to drop the ricotta cheese mixture by teaspoonfuls, lay the noodle on top, and then press down slightly to spread the mixture evenly. I use low-fat ricotta cheese, but feel free to use full-fat ricotta if you like.

MAKES 2 SERVINGS
(ONE 4X8-INCH PAN)

4 ounces gluten-free Italian ground sausage meat or lean ground beef

1¼ cups store-bought gluten-free marinara or homemade Spaghetti Sauce (page 99), divided

½ cup low-fat ricotta cheese or cream cheese alternative

1 large egg

1 cup (4 ounces) shredded mozzarella cheese or cheese alternative, divided

¼ cup plus 1 tablespoon (1.25 ounces) grated Parmesan cheese or soy Parmesan, divided

4 gluten-free lasagna noodles, cooked and cooled

1. Place a rack in the middle of the oven. Preheat the oven to 350°F. Generously grease a 4x8-inch loaf pan.

2. In a heavy skillet, cook the sausage over medium heat until browned and all juices have evaporated, 5 to 7 minutes. Stir in 1 cup of the marinara sauce.

3. In a medium bowl, stir together the ricotta, egg, ½ cup of the mozzarella, and ¼ cup of the Parmesan to make 1 cup.

4. Spread the remaining ¼ cup marinara on the bottom of the pan. Lay 1 noodle on top, then one-third of the ricotta mixture, and one-fourth of the sausage mixture. Repeat twice, ending with the fourth noodle. Top with the remaining sausage mixture, the remaining ½ cup mozzarella, and the remaining 1 tablespoon Parmesan.

5. Cover with foil and bake for 30 minutes. Remove the foil and bake for 10 more minutes, until the cheeses are lightly browned. Let stand on a wire rack for 10 minutes before cutting.

MAKE-AHEAD LASAGNA You can assemble the lasagna the night or morning before serving: Follow the recipe through Step 4. Cover the pan tightly with aluminum foil and refrigerate overnight or all day. When ready to bake, remove the foil and follow Step 5, baking for 50 minutes, until the lasagna is heated through.

Per serving: 770 calories; 47g protein; 38g total fat; 4g fiber; 60g carbohydrates; 216mg cholesterol; 1123mg sodium

Polenta "Lasagna" with Sausage

Polenta is a form of corn grits. Naturally gluten-free, it makes an interesting replacement for pasta in this layered casserole—which can be assembled and refrigerated the day before. Precooked polenta is sold in grocery stores in 18-ounce tubes by Food Merchants and Ancient Harvest. Now, what to do with that leftover tube of polenta? You can store it tightly wrapped, and make the same dish next week. Or dip ½-inch rounds in cornstarch, fry in oil until crispy on both sides, and use as the base (instead of English muffins) for eggs Benedict.

MAKES 2 SERVINGS
(TWO 3¼x5¾-INCH PANS
OR TWO 5-INCH GRATIN
DISHES)

6 ounces gluten-free sweet Italian sausage meat, or 2 links sweet Italian sausage, casings removed

1 cup store-bought marinara sauce or homemade Spaghetti Sauce (page 99)

8¼-inch-thick rounds precooked polenta, cut from an 18-ounce tube

1 cup (4 ounces) shredded mozzarella cheese or cheese alternative

2 tablespoons chopped fresh basil, for garnish

1. Place a rack in the middle position of the oven. Preheat the oven to 400°F. Generously grease two 3¼x5¾-inch nonstick loaf pans (gray, not black) or two 5-inch ovenproof gratin dishes.

2. In a 9-inch skillet, cook the sausage over medium-high heat, breaking up clumps with a knife or fork until the sausage is lightly browned, about 3 minutes.

3. Spread ¼ cup marinara sauce in the bottom of each pan. Arrange 2 polenta slices in a single layer over the sauce in each pan and top with the sausage and ⅓ cup mozzarella cheese. Layer the remaining 2 polenta slices on top and spread evenly with the remaining marinara sauce. Sprinkle with the remaining mozzarella cheese.

4. Bake until the polenta is heated through and the cheese is melted, 15 to 20 minutes. Let stand for 10 minutes. Sprinkle with the basil. To make the lasagna stick together while plating, place a toothpick vertically through each stack. With a thin spatula, carefully transfer the lasagna to dinner plates. Or, serve the lasagna in the baking pans.

Per serving: 590 calories; 29g protein; 41g total fat; 3g fiber; 27g carbohydrates; 116mg cholesterol; 1573mg sodium

Coq au Vin Blanc

Serve this classic French dish in individual bowls, with a side of cooked pasta, rice, or mashed potatoes. A crusty gluten-free French Baguette (page 172) is perfect for sopping up the fragrant sauce.

MAKES 2 SERVINGS

1 slice uncooked bacon

1 teaspoon olive oil

2 boneless, skin-on chicken thighs or 4 chicken legs (about 8 ounces)

½ cup thawed frozen pearl onions, or diced yellow onion

½ cup sliced mushrooms

½ cup ½-inch sliced carrots

⅔ cup dry white wine such as Chardonnay

1 garlic clove, minced

½ to ¾ teaspoon seasoned salt

½ teaspoon dried rosemary, crushed

½ teaspoon dried thyme

¼ teaspoon paprika

¼ teaspoon sugar

¼ teaspoon freshly ground black pepper

1 bay leaf

2 tablespoons chopped fresh parsley, for garnish

1. Place a rack in the middle of the oven. Preheat the oven to 400°F.

2. In a heavy 2-quart saucepan (or a pan just big enough to hold the chicken pieces in a single layer) with a tight-fitting lid, brown the bacon until crisp. Remove the bacon from the pan. Remove the pan from the heat, leaving the bacon drippings in the pan. Reserve the bacon and crumble when cool.

3. Add the olive oil to the bacon drippings. Pat the chicken dry with paper towels, add to the pan, and cook over medium heat until deeply browned on all sides, 7 to 10 minutes. Transfer the chicken to a plate.

4. In the same pan, cook the onions for about 3 minutes, stirring constantly. Add the mushrooms and carrots and sauté 2 minutes more, continuing to stir. Transfer the onions, mushrooms, and carrots to the plate. To the pan, add the remaining ingredients except parsley, and scrape up any browned bits from the pan bottom. Nestle the chicken in a single layer in the pan. Scatter the onions, mushrooms, carrots, and crumbled bacon around the chicken.

5. Cover and bake for 1 hour, until the chicken is tender. Remove the bay leaf. Taste and add more seasoned salt, if desired. Serve in bowls, garnished with the parsley.

Per serving: 260 calories; 29g protein; 6g total fat; 2g fiber; 10g carbohydrates; 68mg cholesterol; 833mg sodium

Oven-Fried Chicken

Even though fried chicken is normally viewed as a meal for several people, it is easily downsized for two. Dredge the pieces and bake while you prepare the rest of the meal. If you like cold fried chicken, double the recipe so you have leftovers.

MAKES 2 SERVINGS

2 tablespoons
brown rice flour

2 tablespoons gluten-free cornmeal

2 teaspoons grated
Parmesan cheese or soy
Parmesan

¼ teaspoon salt

⅛ teaspoon (dash)
freshly ground black
pepper

⅛ teaspoon (dash)
paprika

⅛ teaspoon (dash)
cayenne pepper

⅛ teaspoon (dash) onion
powder

2 large (4- to 5-ounce)
boneless skin-on
chicken thighs

Cooking spray, for
misting

1. Preheat the oven to 400°F. Grease a 9x13-inch nonstick (gray, not black) rimmed baking sheet or line with aluminum foil and grease lightly.

2. In a shallow bowl or a brown paper bag, whisk together the flour, cornmeal, Parmesan, salt, pepper, paprika, cayenne pepper, and onion powder until well combined.

3. Pat the chicken dry with paper towels and dip each thigh into the flour mixture, shaking off any excess. Place the chicken skin side down on the prepared baking sheet.

4. Bake the chicken pieces on one side for 20 minutes. Turn the chicken pieces and gently mist the skin sides with cooking spray to encourage browning. Bake until the chicken registers 165°F when an instant-read thermometer is inserted into the thickest part, 25 to 30 minutes longer (depending on thickness). Serve immediately.

Per serving: 285 calories; 19g protein; 16g total fat; 1g fiber; 16g carbohydrates; 79mg cholesterol; 429mg sodium

Chicken Pot Pies with Rustic Biscuit Crust

This is usually a large dish, designed to serve several people family style, but I've cut it down to two servings, appropriately portioned in 12-ounce ramekins or 5-inch pie pans. I assume that you're using pre-cooked, leftover chicken and vegetables, but if you are starting from scratch, allow extra time to cook them. Pot pies are a whole meal in themselves (meat, starch, vegetable), so I usually serve them with a side of fruit salad and everyone's happy!

MAKES 2 SERVINGS
(TWO 12-OUNCE RAMEKINS OR TWO 5-INCH PIE PANS)

Filling

1 cup diced cooked chicken

½ cup chopped cooked vegetables (broccoli, carrots, celery, corn, and/or peas)

1 small baked russet potato, peeled and diced

¼ cup finely chopped yellow onion

1 tablespoon chopped fresh thyme, or ½ teaspoon dried

1½ teaspoons Dijon mustard

1 teaspoon tomato paste

½ teaspoon gluten-free tamari soy sauce

¼ teaspoon salt

⅛ teaspoon (dash) freshly ground black pepper

1 small garlic clove, minced

1¼ cups gluten-free low-sodium chicken broth

1 tablespoon cornstarch whisked into 1 tablespoon water until smooth

Rustic Biscuit Crust

½ cup Carol's Gluten-Free Flour Blend (page 24)

¼ cup cornstarch or potato starch

1 teaspoon sugar

1 teaspoon baking powder

⅛ teaspoon (dash) baking soda

⅛ teaspoon (dash) xanthan gum

⅛ teaspoon (dash) salt

2 teaspoons chopped fresh thyme, or ¼ teaspoon dried

1 large egg, at room temperature, whisked until foamy

2 tablespoons unsalted butter, buttery spread, or shortening

¼ cup milk of choice, or more as needed

1/16 teaspoon (pinch) paprika, for garnish

1. Preheat the oven to 375°F. Generously grease two 12-ounce ramekins or two 5-inch pie pans (or one 8-inch square baking pan).

2. Make the filling: In a medium bowl, combine all of the filling ingredients except the cornstarch and water. Mix together thoroughly. Stir the cornstarch mixture into the filling until well blended. (It thickens the filling during baking.) Spread the filling in the baking dish(es) and place on a rimmed baking sheet. Cover with foil and bake for 15 minutes, until the filling is heated through.

3. Meanwhile, prepare the biscuit dough: In a food processor, pulse the flour blend, cornstarch, sugar, baking powder, baking soda, xanthan gum, salt, and thyme until thoroughly blended. Reserve 1 tablespoon of the egg. Add the remaining egg to the dry ingredients, along with the butter and milk. Process until the dough is thoroughly blended, scraping down the sides of the bowl with a spatula if necessary. The dough will be somewhat soft and fall easily from a spatula. If it is too stiff, add more milk, a teaspoon at a time, to reach this consistency.

4. Remove the ramekins from the oven, discard the foil, and drop the biscuit dough by tablespoons onto the hot filling. I use a small ice-cream scoop to make equal-sized biscuits. The dough does not have to cover all of the filling; it will spread out as it bakes. Whisk the remaining 1 tablespoon egg with ½ teaspoon water until smooth and then brush it on the biscuit dough to encourage browning. Dust with the paprika. Return the pot pies to the oven and continue baking until the topping is nicely browned, 15 to 20 minutes. Serve immediately.

Per serving: 590 calories; 36g protein; 18g total fat; 4g fiber; 68g carbohydrates; 185mg cholesterol; 1167mg sodium

Middle Eastern Turkey Meatballs over Rice

Sometimes, our taste buds need a jolt, and that's when I turn to Middle Eastern flavors for a change of pace. The feta and mint garnishes add an interesting layer of flavor.

MAKES 2 SERVINGS

Meatballs

8 ounces lean ground turkey

2 tablespoons gluten-free bread crumbs (to make your own, see page 127)

1 large egg

1 tablespoon chopped fresh parsley or 1½ teaspoons dried

1 garlic clove, minced

½ teaspoon ground cumin

¼ teaspoon cinnamon

⅛ teaspoon (dash) crushed red pepper flakes

⅛ teaspoon (dash) salt

⅛ teaspoon (dash) freshly ground black pepper

Tomato Sauce

1 tablespoon olive oil

½ small onion, diced

1 small sprig fresh rosemary, or ½ teaspoon dried

1 teaspoon chopped fresh thyme or ½ teaspoon dried

¼ teaspoon ground cumin

⅛ teaspoon (dash) ground cinnamon

2 (5.5-ounce) cans tomato juice (about 1¼ cups)

2 tablespoons orange juice

¼ teaspoon sugar

⅛ teaspoon (dash) salt

⅛ teaspoon (dash) freshly ground black pepper

1½ cups hot cooked brown or white rice

Feta cheese and chopped fresh mint, for garnish

1. Place a rack in the middle of the oven. Preheat the oven to 350°F. Line a 9x13-inch rimmed baking sheet with aluminum foil.

2. Make the meatballs: In a medium bowl, combine all of the meatball ingredients and mix well with your hands. Shape into 8 meatballs, about 2 tablespoons each and 1½ inches in diameter. Place the meatballs on the baking sheet and bake until browned, about 15 minutes.

3. While the meatballs bake, make the sauce: Heat the oil in a medium lidded skillet over medium heat. Add the onion and cook until slightly softened, about 3 minutes. Add the rosemary, thyme, cumin, and cinnamon and cook, stirring, for 1 minute. Add the tomato juice, orange juice, sugar, salt, and pepper and stir to blend thoroughly. Reduce the heat to low and simmer, covered, for 20 minutes.

4. Add the baked meatballs to the sauce and bring to serving temperature. Serve in bowls over the rice, garnished with feta cheese and mint.

MAKE-AHEAD MEATBALLS To make and freeze meatballs to use later, follow the recipe through Step 2. Cool, and then freeze in a plastic container or zipper-top freezer bag. To use the meatballs, thaw overnight in the refrigerator, then add to the tomato sauce and bring to serving temperature.

Per serving: 485 calories; 32g protein; 17g total fat; 4g fiber; 49g carbohydrates; 167mg cholesterol; 720mg sodium

Chicken Tikka Masala

Tikka Masala is an Indian dish that can be made in many different ways, but is technically just chicken simmered in a spicy sauce. My simple version, served over rice, is a meal in a bowl, perhaps accompanied by some sliced fresh fruit to complement the spicy notes.

MAKES 2 SERVINGS

1 tablespoon canola oil

¼ cup diced onion

2 small garlic cloves, minced

1 (1-inch) piece peeled fresh ginger, grated; or 1 teaspoon ground ginger

½ teaspoon garam masala, or ¾ teaspoon for more spice

¼ teaspoon smoked paprika

1 (14.5-ounce) can fire-roasted tomatoes, undrained

½ pound boneless, skinless chicken thighs or breasts, cut into ½-inch cubes

¼ cup plain yogurt or milk of choice

¼ teaspoon crushed red pepper flakes

¼ teaspoon salt

⅛ teaspoon (dash) freshly ground black pepper

1 cup frozen shelled raw edamame, or frozen green peas

1½ cups hot cooked brown, jasmine, or basmati rice

2 tablespoons chopped fresh cilantro, for garnish

1. In a medium saucepan, heat the oil over medium heat. Add the onion, garlic, and ginger and cook, stirring constantly, for 1 minute. Add the garam masala and paprika and cook, stirring constantly, for 30 seconds.

2. Transfer the mixture to a blender, add the tomatoes, and puree until the sauce is smooth. (Or, leave the mixture in the saucepan and puree with an immersion blender until smooth.) Return the sauce to the skillet and add the chicken, yogurt, red pepper flakes, salt, and pepper. Bring to a boil and reduce the heat to medium-low. Cover and cook until the chicken is cooked through, 12 to 15 minutes. Stir in the edamame and simmer, uncovered, another 5 minutes.

3. Divide the rice among 2 bowls and top with the chicken and sauce. Serve, garnished with cilantro.

Per serving: 685 calories; 41g protein; 28g total fat; 14g fiber; 76g carbohydrates; 4mg cholesterol; 590mg sodium

Chicken Cacciatore

Also called Hunter's Stew, this famous Italian dish is rich and hearty. The sauce is rustically coarse; for a smoother version, puree the tomatoes in a food processor or blender. A crisp garden salad and gluten-free Focaccia (page 169) make it a meal.

MAKES 2 SERVINGS

4 chicken legs or 2 bone-in chicken thighs (about 8 ounces total)

1 tablespoon olive oil

1 (14-ounce) can whole tomatoes, chopped or crushed, or pureed

¼ cup white wine or gluten-free low-sodium chicken broth

¼ cup diced onion

¼ cup diced green, red, or yellow bell pepper

1 tablespoon tomato paste

1 small garlic clove, minced

¾ teaspoon seasoned salt

½ teaspoon Italian seasoning

⅛ teaspoon (dash) freshly ground black pepper

⅛ teaspoon (dash) crushed red pepper flakes

1⁄16 teaspoon (pinch) sugar

6 ounces hot, cooked gluten-free pasta (penne, rigatoni, or other spiral pasta)

Fresh basil or parsley, for garnish

1. Pat the chicken dry with paper towels. In a heavy 2-quart saucepan, heat the oil over medium heat. Add the chicken in two batches and cook until lightly browned on all sides, about 5 minutes. Transfer to a plate.

2. To the pan, add the remaining ingredients except pasta and basil. Stir to blend together, scraping the pan to release any browned bits.

3. Nestle the chicken pieces in the sauce so they are covered, cover the pan, and simmer over medium-low heat until the chicken is tender, about 30 minutes. For a thicker sauce, remove the lid and simmer for another 5 to 10 minutes to reduce the sauce. Serve over bowls of hot cooked pasta, garnished with fresh basil or parsley.

MEASURING SHORT-CUT PASTA An easy guide is that 2 ounces of uncooked penne pasta is a generous ½ cup, which cooks up into a heaping cup of cooked pasta. When I cook short-cut pasta (such as penne, fusilli, or macaroni) for two people, I simply measure a generous cup of the dry pasta. For smaller cuts of pasta such as ditalini, ⅓ cup of uncooked pasta equals 2 ounces.

Per serving: 340 calories; 20g protein; 10g total fat; 4g fiber; 39g carbohydrates; 54mg cholesterol; 932mg sodium

Arroz con Pollo

Despite the exotic name, this is simply chicken cooked with rice and saffron—very popular in Spain and the Mediterranean. It is an all-in-one meal in itself, so just add a salad and gluten-free bread.

MAKES 2 SERVINGS

2 boneless, skinless chicken thighs (about 8 ounces total)

2 tablespoons cornstarch

1 tablespoon olive oil

2 tablespoons diced onion

2 tablespoons diced green bell pepper

1 cup gluten-free low-sodium chicken broth

1 cup canned whole tomatoes, chopped but undrained

2 tablespoons dry sherry or white wine

⅓ cup long-grain white rice

½ cup chopped mushrooms

1 small garlic clove, minced

½ teaspoon seasoned salt or plain salt

¼ teaspoon freshly ground black pepper

¹⁄₁₆ teaspoon (pinch) crushed red pepper flakes

¹⁄₁₆ teaspoon (pinch) crushed saffron threads

1 small bay leaf

¼ cup frozen green peas

2 tablespoons chopped fresh parsley, for garnish

1. Place a rack in the middle position of the oven. Preheat the oven to 375°F.

2. Pat the chicken dry with paper towels and dredge both sides in the cornstarch. In a 10-inch heavy oven-proof skillet with a tight-fitting lid, heat the oil over medium heat. Add the chicken and cook until lightly browned on both sides, about 5 minutes. Transfer the chicken to a plate.

3. Add the onion and bell pepper to the skillet and cook over medium heat, stirring occasionally, until the onion is lightly browned, 3 to 5 minutes. Add the broth, tomatoes, sherry, rice, mushrooms, garlic, seasoned salt, black pepper, red pepper flakes, saffron, and bay leaf. Stir to combine. Nestle the chicken in the rice mixture.

4. Cover and bake for 30 minutes. Add the peas and continue baking, covered, another 10 minutes, until the chicken is tender and the rice is absorbed. Remove the bay leaf and serve, garnished with the parsley.

Per serving: 370 calories; 23g protein; 10g total fat; 3g fiber; 44g carbohydrates; 54mg cholesterol; 862mg sodium

Paella

As I learned when I visited Spain, there are many different kinds of paella—depending on the region. My version is simple yet flavorful and a meal in itself, so the portions are large. I serve it with a tossed green salad and a gluten-free French Baguette (page 172).

MAKES 2 SERVINGS

4 ounces chorizo (1 link), cut into ¼-inch slices (or crumbled if using raw chorizo)

1 teaspoon olive oil

6 ounces skinless chicken (1 boneless thigh or boneless breast half), cut into ¼-inch strips

¾ cup canned diced tomatoes, undrained

1½ cups gluten-free low-sodium chicken broth

⅓ cup uncooked Arborio or other short-grain white rice

1 tablespoon dried onion

1 medium garlic clove, minced

1 teaspoon paprika

¾ teaspoon dried oregano

⅛ teaspoon (dash) salt

⅛ teaspoon (dash) crushed saffron threads

¹⁄₁₆ teaspoon (pinch) cayenne

6 large raw shrimp (31 to 35 count), peeled and deveined, tails on

¼ cup frozen green peas

Salt and freshly ground black pepper, to taste

2 teaspoons chopped fresh parsley, for garnish

1. In a 10-inch nonstick skillet with a lid, cook the chorizo over medium heat until lightly browned, about 2 minutes. Transfer the chorizo to a plate. Keeping the heat at medium, heat the oil in the skillet, then add the chicken. Cook until lightly browned on all sides, about 3 minutes. Transfer the chicken to the plate with the chorizo.

2. To the now-empty skillet, add the tomatoes, broth, rice, dried onion, garlic, paprika, oregano, salt, saffron, and cayenne. Stir, bring to a boil, reduce the heat to low, and simmer, covered, for 15 minutes.

3. Nestle the chicken and chorizo in the rice mixture in the skillet. Cover and simmer for 10 minutes. Arrange the shrimp and peas in the rice mixture, pushing down to submerge them, and cook another 5 minutes, uncovered, until the shrimp are cooked through and the liquid is absorbed. Taste and add salt and pepper, if desired. Serve immediately, garnished with fresh parsley.

Per serving: 560 calories; 42g protein; 27g total fat; 2g fiber; 36g carbohydrates; 147mg cholesterol; 1491mg sodium

Shrimp and Grits with Sausage

This is Southern comfort food at its best, and fairly quick as well. I prefer Bob's Red Mill corn grits/polenta because of its lovely golden color and hearty texture—and I know it's gluten free. It cooks in the microwave quickly. Sometimes, I cook thin strips of red bell pepper with the sausage for a little extra color and texture.

MAKES 2 SERVINGS

1¾ cups water

⅓ cup Bob's Red Mill gluten-free yellow corn grits/polenta

¼ teaspoon salt, or to taste

½ cup (2 ounces) shredded cheddar cheese (mild or sharp, your choice)

1 teaspoon butter or buttery spread

2 teaspoons olive oil

2 tablespoons finely chopped onion

3 to 4 ounces gluten-free Andouille sausage (1 link), cut into ¼-inch coins

½ pound large shrimp (31 to 35 count), peeled, deveined, and tails removed

¼ cup gluten-free low-sodium chicken broth

1 small garlic clove, minced

⅛ teaspoon (dash) hot sauce, or to taste

1 small green onion, including green tops, sliced very thin, for garnish

1. In a medium microwave-safe bowl, whisk the water, grits, and salt together. (I use a 4-cup Pyrex measuring cup, which is large enough to avoid boil-overs.) Lay a sheet of wax paper over the bowl and microwave on High in two 3-minute increments, whisking between each increment, until the polenta is slightly firm and no lumps remain. Stir in the cheese and butter. Keep warm.

2. Meanwhile, heat the olive oil in a medium heavy skillet over medium heat. Add the onion and sausage and cook until the sausage is lightly browned on both sides and the onion is translucent, about 4 minutes. Stir in the shrimp, broth, garlic, and hot sauce and cook for 2 to 3 minutes, just until the shrimp turn pink.

3. Divide the grits between 2 bowls. Add the shrimp mixture and juices and serve, garnished with the green onion.

Per serving: 510 calories; 41g protein; 26g total fat; 4g fiber; 25g carbohydrates; 235mg cholesterol; 971mg sodium

Peanut Sesame Noodles with Shrimp

This dish is good hot or cold, and you can vary the vegetables using whatever you like to equal 1½ cups. It is prettiest with a variety of colorful vegetables, but use what you have on hand. I usually use cooked shrimp from the freezer, but diced cooked chicken also works well.

MAKES 2 SERVINGS

4 ounces gluten-free spaghetti or fettuccine (see Measuring Spaghetti, page 98)

1 cup snow peas, halved

½ red bell pepper, seeded and cut into ⅛-inch slivers

¼ cup orange juice

¼ cup creamy peanut butter

2 tablespoons gluten-free tamari soy sauce

1 tablespoon rice vinegar

1 teaspoon sesame oil

1 teaspoon grated fresh ginger

$\frac{1}{16}$ teaspoon (pinch) hot sauce, or to taste

10 large cooked medium shrimp, peeled and deveined (41 to 50 count)

1 tablespoon chopped salted shelled peanuts, for garnish

1 green onion, including green tops, sliced, for garnish

1. Cook the pasta in boiling, salted water according to package directions until al dente. When the pasta is 3 minutes from being done, add the snow peas and bell pepper and cook until crisp-tender. Drain the pasta and vegetables in a sieve, reserving ¼ cup of the pasta water in a cup. Return the pasta to the pot.

2. Meanwhile, make the sauce: In a small pan, whisk together the orange juice, peanut butter, tamari, vinegar, sesame oil, ginger, and hot sauce. Cook over medium heat, stirring constantly, until the sauce is smooth, about 3 to 5 minutes. If it's too thick, add some pasta water to thin it.

3. Add the shrimp to the cooked pasta and vegetables in the pot. Add the sauce and toss until well coated. Serve immediately, garnished with the peanuts and green onion.

Per serving: 530 calories; 25g protein; 23g total fat; 6g fiber; 60g carbohydrates; 46mg cholesterol; 807mg sodium

Shrimp Creole

I always have a bag of frozen shrimp stashed in my freezer so I can use as much (or as little) as I need, keeping the rest frozen for the next meal. We like shrimp Creole on white rice, but you can use other varieties such as jasmine, basmati, or brown rice.

MAKES 2 SERVINGS

2 teaspoons olive oil

½ cup diced green bell pepper

½ cup finely chopped celery

¼ cup diced onion

1 (14-ounce) can whole tomatoes, undrained

1 small garlic clove, minced

¼ teaspoon chili powder, or to taste

¼ teaspoon sugar

¼ teaspoon gluten-free Worcestershire sauce

2 drops hot pepper sauce, or to taste

1 small bay leaf

½ pound medium-large shrimp (36 to 40 count), peeled and deveined

Salt and freshly ground black pepper, to taste (optional)

1 teaspoon cornstarch stirred into 1 tablespoon cold water, if needed

1½ cups hot cooked white rice

2 tablespoons chopped fresh parsley

1. In a medium, heavy 2-quart saucepan, heat the oil over medium heat. Add the bell pepper, celery, and onion and cook until just tender. Add the tomatoes, garlic, chili powder, sugar, Worcestershire sauce, hot pepper sauce, and bay leaf. Simmer, uncovered, for 20 to 30 minutes to reduce the sauce a bit.

2. Add the shrimp, cover, and simmer another 5 minutes, until the shrimp are cooked and heated through. Taste and add salt and pepper, if desired. If the sauce needs thickening, stir in the cornstarch mixture. Cook, stirring, until the mixture thickens slightly. Discard the bay leaf. Serve over hot cooked rice, garnished with parsley.

Per serving: 410 calories; 30g protein; 7g total fat; 4g fiber; 56g carbohydrates; 172mg cholesterol; 508mg sodium

Coconut-Curry Salmon with Edamame

In this easy Asian-themed recipe, salmon and vegetables quickly simmer in a coconut milk sauce. The dish begs for your innovation. Instead of tomatoes, you might use slender strips of red bell pepper. Instead of edamame, maybe snow peas or green peas. I prefer brown rice, but jasmine or basmati also work nicely. This recipe comes together very quickly if you start with cooked rice.

MAKES 2 SERVINGS

½ (15-ounce) can low-fat coconut milk (¾ cup)

1 tablespoon packed brown sugar

Juice of 1 lime (about 2 teaspoons)

2 teaspoons red curry paste, or 3 teaspoons for a spicier dish

2 (5-ounce) salmon fillets or steaks, skinned if desired

¼ teaspoon salt

⅛ teaspoon (dash) freshly ground black pepper

½ cup frozen shelled edamame, thawed

6 grape or cherry tomatoes, halved

2 tablespoons chopped fresh cilantro, divided

1½ cups hot cooked rice (brown, or jasmine or basmati)

1. In an 8-inch saucepan with 2-inch sides (or just big enough to hold the salmon in a single layer), stir together the coconut milk, sugar, lime juice, and curry paste until smooth. Sprinkle the salmon with the salt and pepper and gently lay it in the sauce. Scatter the edamame, tomatoes, and 1 tablespoon of the cilantro in the sauce around the salmon.

2. Place the saucepan over medium heat and bring to a gentle simmer. Reduce the heat to medium-low, cover, and simmer until the salmon flakes easily and is cooked through, 8 to 10 minutes (depending on the thickness of the salmon).

3. Divide the rice between two large soup bowls. Top with the salmon and vegetables and pour the sauce on top. Serve, garnished with the remaining 1 tablespoon cilantro.

LEFTOVER COCONUT MILK Use the remaining half-can of coconut milk in a smoothie or as the base for Vanilla Pudding (page 220) or Chocolate Pudding (page 217).

Per serving: 655 calories; 49g protein; 24g total fat; 8g fiber; 60g carbohydrates; 75mg cholesterol; 527mg sodium

Baked Fish in Parchment

This method of cooking is particularly adaptable for two, because you make two individual packets. Use any fish you like in this easy dish (I like salmon) and any herb. I'm partial to dill, basil, or thyme but use what you have. In fact, you can put anything you like in this parchment packet if it all cooks in about the same amount of time. You can assemble the packets the night before and just pop them in the oven when it is dinnertime. If you don't have parchment paper, use aluminum foil. The presentation won't be quite as pretty, but foil is very functional.

MAKES 2 SERVINGS

2 (5-ounce) skinless boneless fish fillets (such as salmon, cod, or red snapper)

½ teaspoon salt

½ teaspoon freshly ground black pepper

2 teaspoons chopped fresh dill, basil, or thyme, or ½ teaspoon dried

2 tablespoons chopped grape or cherry tomatoes or sun-dried tomatoes

2 canned marinated artichoke halves, coarsely chopped

1 stalk green vegetable such as broccoli, cut into ¼-inch strips

½ small red or yellow bell pepper, seeded and cut into ⅛-inch slices

2 tablespoons capers (optional)

1 tablespoon red wine vinegar

2 teaspoons olive oil

⅛ teaspoon (dash) sugar

1. Preheat the oven to 425°F.

2. Lay two 12-inch squares of parchment paper on a flat surface and place a fillet in the center of each. Sprinkle evenly with the salt and pepper. Arrange the herbs, tomatoes, artichokes, green vegetable, bell pepper, and capers (if using) on the fillets. In a small bowl, whisk the vinegar, oil, and sugar together until smooth; pour the sauce over each fillet.

3. For each packet, bring two edges of the parchment paper together. Fold the edges down by ½-inch, crease sharply, and continue folding down in ½-inch turns until the fold is flush with the food. Twist the unfolded ends together to seal tightly and hold in the juices. Place the packets, folded side up, on a rimmed baking sheet.

continued~

4. Bake the packets for 12 to 15 minutes. The packets will puff up and brown. Place each packet on a serving plate. Slowly cut open the packets with kitchen scissors to allow steam to release gently, wearing kitchen gloves to avoid steam burns. The fish is done if it is opaque and flakes easily with a fork. (Or with a spatula, gently remove the fish and vegetables from the parchment and transfer to serving plates.) Serve.

MAKE-AHEAD PACKETS You can make the packets up to 24 hours ahead of time—place the assembled packets on a large plate and refrigerate. When ready, bake in the preheated oven as directed in Step 2, but the chilled packets will take longer, 15 to 20 minutes.

Per serving: 190 calories; 27g protein; 6g total fat; 2g fiber; 5g carbohydrates; 61mg cholesterol; 779mg sodium

Crab Cakes

At our house, we love crab cakes so much that we have them at least twice a month. And they are always served at our annual seafood dinner on New Year's Eve. I find it easiest to buy the 8-ounce tub of Phillips brand crab meat (rather than shelling whole crab legs myself). I use half of the container for this recipe, freezing the rest for a later meal of crab cakes.

MAKES 2 SERVINGS
(2 CRAB CAKES EACH)

¼ cup gluten-free bread crumbs (to make your own, see page 127)

2 tablespoons mayonnaise or mayonnaise alternative

1 large egg

Juice of 1 lemon

1 tablespoon chopped fresh parsley, or 1 teaspoon dried

1 teaspoon dried minced onion

1 teaspoon Old Bay seasoning

¼ teaspoon salt

¼ teaspoon freshly ground black pepper

4 ounces (half of an 8-ounce container) lump crab meat

1 tablespoon canola oil

Cocktail sauce, for serving

1. Place a rack in the middle of the oven. Preheat the oven to 425°F. Lightly oil a 10-inch oven-proof skillet.

2. In a medium bowl, whisk together the bread crumbs, mayonnaise, egg, lemon juice, parsley, dried onion, Old Bay, salt, and pepper. Gently stir in the crab until evenly mixed. Shape into four cakes, patting into 3-inch rounds with your hands.

3. Place the crab cakes in the skillet and cook over medium heat until they are lightly browned on the bottom, about 5 minutes. Carefully turn the crab cakes over and transfer the skillet to the oven. Bake for another 10 minutes, or just until the crab cakes are cooked through. Serve with the cocktail sauce.

MAKE-AHEAD CRAB CAKES You can make the crab cakes up to a day ahead of time. Follow the recipe through Step 2, then cover and refrigerate. To finish, cook as directed in Step 3.

Per serving: 300 calories; 15g protein; 22g total fat; 1g fiber; 12g carbohydrates; 143mg cholesterol; 689mg sodium

Sheet Pan Supper of Roasted Fish and Vegetables

Making meals the sheet pan way works especially well when cooking for two people because an entire meal fits on one 9x13-inch pan. You begin roasting the food that takes longest to cook (such as potatoes), then add additional foods (fish and vegetables) later, since they cook faster. If your vegetables are especially delicate or if you prefer them steamed (not roasted), layer them under the fish.

MAKES 2 SERVINGS

½ pound small Yukon gold potatoes (about 6) or fingerlings, halved (2 cups)

1 tablespoon olive oil

¾ teaspoon dried herbs of your choice (I like oregano or tarragon), divided

¼ teaspoon smoked paprika

2 (5-ounce salmon) fillets, skinned if desired

1 cup thin asparagus cut into ½-inch pieces

½ cup cherry or grape tomatoes, halved

¼ teaspoon salt

⅛ teaspoon (dash) freshly ground black pepper

1 fresh lemon, cut into wedges, for serving

1. Place a rack in the middle of the oven. Preheat the oven to 425°F. Line a 9x13-inch nonstick (gray, not black) rimmed baking sheet with foil; lightly grease the foil. Or grease a 10-inch ovenproof skillet.

2. In a medium bowl, toss the potatoes with the olive oil, ¼ teaspoon of the herbs, and the paprika until well coated. Arrange evenly, cut sides down, on the baking sheet or in the skillet and roast for 20 minutes.

3. Arrange the salmon, asparagus, and tomatoes on top of the potatoes and sprinkle with the remaining ½ teaspoon herbs and the salt and pepper. Continue to roast until the salmon is cooked through and the potatoes are tender, 10 to 15 minutes, depending on thickness of the fish. Serve with lemon wedges, for squeezing.

Variations: You can alter this meal to what you have on hand. For example, make a similar meal with interesting variety by using cod instead of salmon, ⅛-inch red bell pepper strips instead of tomatoes, and/or broccoli florets or snow peas instead of asparagus. Monitor the roasting times accordingly. Generally speaking, the thinner and less dense the food, the shorter the cooking time. A good rule of thumb is to put the more delicate vegetables under the fish.

Per serving: 345 calories; 33g protein; 12g total fat; 4g fiber; 29g carbohydrates; 74mg cholesterol; 374mg sodium

Mediterranean Tuna with Chickpea Salad

This dish makes a lovely cold supper for a warm summer night. Serve with gluten-free crackers followed by a dessert of frozen sorbet and store-bought gluten-free cookies.

MAKES 2 SERVINGS

Salad
1 (14.5-ounce) can chickpeas or cannellini beans, thoroughly rinsed and drained

1 medium tomato, seeded and diced, or ½ cup diced red bell pepper

¼ chopped pitted Kalamata olives

¼ cup chopped English (hothouse) cucumber

1 garlic clove, minced

2 tablespoons chopped fresh mint

2 tablespoons chopped fresh parsley

Salt and freshly ground black pepper, to taste

Dressing
2 tablespoons red wine vinegar

½ teaspoon Dijon mustard

⅛ teaspoon (dash) salt, or more to taste

¼ teaspoon freshly ground black pepper

2 tablespoons extra-virgin olive oil

1 (5-ounce) can chunk light tuna in water, drained

2 tablespoons feta cheese, for garnish

Chopped parsley, for garnish

1. Make the salad: In a medium bowl, toss together the chickpeas, tomato, olives, cucumber, garlic, mint, and parsley until well blended. Season with salt and pepper.

2. Make the dressing: In a small bowl, whisk together the vinegar, mustard, salt, and pepper until smooth, then whisk in the olive oil in a slow, steady stream until the dressing thickens. Or, shake in a small jar until the dressing thickens.

3. Toss the dressing with the chickpea mixture. Refrigerate for a few hours to meld flavors.

4. To serve, let the salad stand at room temperature for 20 minutes. Taste and add more salt and pepper, if desired. Gently stir in the tuna with a spatula. Serve, garnished with the feta cheese and parsley.

WHITE BEANS For a flavor variation, or if you don't have chickpeas on hand, substitute cannellini (white kidney) beans for the chickpeas.

Per serving: 615 calories; 22g protein; 30g total fat; 19g fiber; 69g carbohydrates; 9mg cholesterol; 758mg sodium

Tuna-Noodle Casserole

I like to make my own soup for this comforting casserole with the easy recipe below—the richer the milk, the creamier the casserole. But if you tolerate dairy, you can use 1 cup of a store-bought gluten-free cream of mushroom soup (most store-bought versions contain dairy), undiluted. Canned mushrooms produce a lighter color while fresh mushrooms might make the sauce darker.

MAKES 2 SERVINGS
(TWO 4-INCH, 8-OUNCE RAMEKINS OR
ONE 4X8-INCH BAKING DISH)

¼ cup finely chopped mushrooms

1 tablespoon unsalted butter or buttery spread

1 tablespoon sweet rice flour, or 1½ teaspoons cornstarch

1 cup milk of choice, divided

¼ teaspoon gluten-free instant chicken base or bouillon

1 tablespoon dried minced onion

⅛ teaspoon (dash) celery salt

1/16 teaspoon (pinch) freshly ground black pepper

1 (5-ounce) can low-sodium chunk light tuna in water, drained

4 ounces gluten-free pasta (elbow macaroni, spiral, or penne), cooked (about 1½ cups)

¼ cup green peas

2 tablespoons gluten-free bread crumbs (to make your own, page 127)

Cooking spray

1/16 teaspoon (pinch) paprika, for garnish

1. Preheat the oven to 350°F. Grease two 4-inch glass (Pyrex) ramekins or one 4x8-inch baking dish.

2. In a small saucepan over medium heat, cook the mushrooms in the butter for 1 minute. Put the sweet rice flour in a small measuring cup and slowly whisk in ¼ cup of the milk until smooth. Whisk in the remaining milk, the chicken base, dried onion, celery salt, and pepper. Add this mixture to the mushrooms and cook, stirring constantly, until the soup thickens, 1 to 2 minutes.

3. In a large bowl, toss together the tuna (breaking up any chunks), pasta, and peas. Add the soup and toss until well blended. Spread evenly in the prepared dish(es) and sprinkle with the bread crumbs. Coat the crumbs with cooking spray to encourage browning.

4. Bake until hot and bubbly around the edges, 15 to 20 minutes. Serve hot, garnished with the paprika.

Per serving: 375 calories; 28g protein; 9g total fat; 3g fiber; 47g carbohydrates; 49mg cholesterol; 360mg sodium

Easy Weeknight Pasta ⓥ

I save this basic quick dish for nights when I want something hot, yet meat-free and light. If you're a fresh basil lover, as I am, you can use as much as you like: Start with 1 tablespoon and go from there—you can always add more! For extra color and crunch, add chopped bell pepper or green onions, olives, or artichoke hearts—or perhaps pepperoni slices for more protein if you are not vegetarian. A crisp garden salad rounds out this simple meal.

MAKES 2 SERVINGS

2 tablespoons extra-virgin olive oil, divided

1 large garlic clove, minced

¼ teaspoon crushed red pepper

¼ cup gluten-free bread crumbs (to make your own, see right)

4 ounces (1 cup) gluten-free spiral pasta

1 tablespoon chopped fresh basil or 1 teaspoon dried

¼ cup (1 ounce) grated Parmesan cheese, or to taste

Salt and freshly ground black pepper (optional)

2 plum tomatoes, finely chopped

2 tablespoons chopped fresh parsley, for garnish

1 lemon, halved

1. In a medium skillet, heat 1 tablespoon of the oil over low heat. Add the garlic and crushed red pepper and cook for 1 minute, stirring constantly. Add the bread crumbs and cook, stirring constantly, just until they start to lightly brown. Set aside.

2. In a medium pot of boiling, salted water, cook the pasta according to package directions until al dente. Drain the pasta in a sieve, leaving 2 tablespoons of hot water in the pot. Return the pasta to the pot and add the remaining 1 tablespoon oil, the bread crumb mixture, basil, and Parmesan. Toss gently and season with salt and pepper, if desired.

3. Divide the pasta among two serving bowls and serve, topped with the chopped tomatoes, a sprinkle of parsley, and the lemon halves.

Per serving: 350 calories; 11g protein; 9g total fat; 4g fiber; 58g carbohydrates; 2 mg cholesterol; 172mg sodium

Homemade Gluten-Free Bread Crumbs

I once watched a chef demonstrate a dish for a gluten-free audience. As he nonchalantly tossed a leftover slice of gluten-free bread into the garbage, the crowd uttered a collective gasp. "How could he throw away gluten-free bread?" At my house, any leftover or stale bread is immediately whirled into bread crumbs in my mini food processor and stored in the freezer. Although I can buy gluten-free bread crumbs in grocery stores, it is much cheaper and better tasting to make my own. If I keep my stash of bread crumbs in the freezer, they don't go stale and they are always available, especially in the small amounts called for in this book. So, I suggest you make your own. Here's how to do it.

Start with bread torn into small pieces; you'll need about 4 cups. If you want to make Italian bread crumbs, add 1 teaspoon onion powder and 4 teaspoons dried Italian seasoning. Pulse on and off in a food processor until the crumbs reach the desired consistency. For bread crumbs that are lighter in color and that brown uniformly, cut the crusts from the bread before processing. This amount of bread will make about 2 cups of bread crumbs.

Store bread crumbs tightly covered in the refrigerator for up to 2 weeks, or freeze for up to 3 months. Keep these on hand for all sorts of recipes including Crab Cakes (page 121), Spaghetti and Meatballs (page 99), and Meat Loaf (page 82).

Pasta Primavera

(V)

Prep everything before you start cooking and this dish will come together quickly. Primavera means springtime, so I use spring vegetables such as asparagus, but use whatever vegetables you like. For non-vegetarians, add cooked shrimp or chicken.

MAKES 2 SERVINGS

4 ounces (1 cup) uncooked gluten-free penne or other short-cut pasta

½ cup 1-inch cut asparagus

¼ cup sliced yellow squash

¼ cup ⅛-inch sliced red bell pepper

¼ cup green peas

1 teaspoon grated lemon zest

3 tablespoons lemon juice

1 small shallot, very finely diced

1 tablespoon olive oil

⅛ teaspoon (dash) salt

⅛ teaspoon (dash) freshly ground black pepper

1/16 teaspoon (pinch) crushed red pepper, or to taste

1 tablespoon grated Parmesan or soy Parmesan, for garnish

Chopped fresh parsley, for garnish

1. In a medium pot of boiling, salted water, cook the pasta according to package directions until al dente. Drain the pasta and return to the pot; it will continue to cook while it sits.

2. Meanwhile, bring a small pot of salted water to a boil. Add the asparagus, squash, bell pepper, and peas and cook for 2 to 3 minutes, or just until slightly softened but still crisp. If you like softer vegetables, cook them to your liking. Drain the vegetables and plunge into ice water to stop the cooking and preserve the color. Drain again.

3. In a small bowl, make the dressing: Whisk together the lemon zest, lemon juice, shallot, olive oil, salt, black pepper, and crushed red pepper until well blended.

4. Add the vegetables and the dressing to the pasta and toss until coated thoroughly. Serve, garnished with Parmesan and parsley.

Per serving: 315 calories; 10g protein; 8g total fat; 5g fiber; 51g carbohydrates; 2mg cholesterol; 183mg sodium

Macaroni and Cheese

This is honest-to-goodness down-home cooking . . . at a size that's right for you. Serve it in two ramekins or couple-style in an 8-inch casserole dish. Either way, it brings out the kid in all of us. You can use mild or sharp cheddar cheese. I prefer sharp because it is more flavorful, although it does not melt quite as smoothly; use the cheese that works for you.

MAKES 2 SERVINGS
(TWO 4-INCH RAMEKINS
OR ONE 8-INCH
CASSEROLE)

4 ounces (1 cup) uncooked gluten-free elbow macaroni

1 tablespoon unsalted butter or buttery spread

1 teaspoon sweet rice flour, or 1¼ teaspoons cornstarch

1 cup milk of choice, divided

1 cup plus 2 tablespoons (about 4½ ounces) shredded cheddar cheese or cheese alternative

½ teaspoon dry mustard (optional)

¼ teaspoon salt

1/16 teaspoon (pinch) freshly ground black pepper

Paprika, for garnish

2 teaspoons chopped fresh parsley, for garnish

1. Place a rack in the middle of the oven. Preheat the oven to 350°F. Generously grease two 4-inch glass (Pyrex) ramekins or one 8-inch glass or ceramic baking dish.

2. In a medium pot of boiling, salted water, cook the macaroni according to package directions until tender. Drain, return to the pot, and set aside.

3. In a small saucepan, melt the butter over medium heat. In a measuring cup, whisk the sweet rice flour into ¼ cup of the milk until smooth, and then whisk in the remaining milk. Add to the pan and cook, whisking constantly, until slightly thickened and bubbly, 5 to 7 minutes. Stir in 1 cup of the cheese and the mustard, salt, and pepper until smooth.

4. Pour the sauce over the macaroni in the pot and toss to coat thoroughly. Divide between the ramekins or spread in the baking dish. Sprinkle with the remaining 2 tablespoons cheese.

5. Bake for 20 minutes, or just until bubbly around the edges. Let stand 10 minutes before serving, garnished with a sprinkle of paprika and parsley.

Per serving: 570 calories; 27g protein; 38g total fat; 2g fiber; 50g carbohydrates; 87mg cholesterol; 724mg sodium

Chiles Rellenos Casserole ⓥ

From-scratch Chiles Rellenos are notoriously time-consuming to make, so enjoy the flavors in this easy casserole without the fuss. It is perfect for lunch, Sunday brunch, or a light supper. Add ½ cup diced cooked chicken for the non-vegetarians. A crisp tossed salad and corn tortillas make perfect accompaniments. For a spicier dish, increase the green chiles to 3 or 4 tablespoons. For best results, start with the ingredients at room temperature.

MAKES 2 SERVINGS (ONE 4x8-INCH LOAF)

½ cup (2 ounces) shredded Monterey Jack cheese or cheese alternative

½ cup (2 ounces) shredded cheddar cheese or cheese alternative, plus 1 tablespoon for sprinkling

½ cup sour cream or sour cream alternative

2 large eggs

2 tablespoons diced green chiles (from a 4-ounce can)

1 teaspoon chopped fresh oregano or ¼ teaspoon dried, or to taste

$\frac{1}{16}$ teaspoon (pinch) ground cumin (optional)

⅛ teaspoon (dash) paprika

2 tablespoons chopped fresh cilantro, for garnish

1. Place a rack in the middle of the oven. Preheat the oven to 350°F. Generously grease a 4x8-inch loaf pan.

2. In a small bowl, whisk together the cheeses, sour cream, eggs, chiles, oregano, and cumin (if using); or blend with an electric mixer on low speed. Pour the mixture into the pan and sprinkle with the remaining 1 tablespoon cheddar. Dust lightly with the paprika.

3. Bake for 30 to 35 minutes, until the top is puffy and golden brown. Serve immediately, garnished with cilantro.

LEFTOVER GREEN CHILES Store the leftover diced green chiles in a tightly closed screw-top glass jar so that the strong green chile smell does not permeate your refrigerator. They can be added to scrambled eggs, frittatas, stews, and chili.

Per serving: 310 calories; 21g protein; 23g total fat; 1g fiber; 4g carbohydrates; 246mg cholesterol; 414mg sodium

Preparation time: 10 minutes
Chilling time: 8 hours (optional)
Baking time: 25 minutes

Layered Bean-Tortilla Casserole

With its hearty beans, this casserole is a filling vegetarian main dish. But if you want to make it even heartier for non-vegetarians, add ½ cup of cooked diced chicken or pork—or cooked ground beef. And feel free to vary the ingredient proportions, for example, using more cheese. If you are extra hungry, make a casserole for each of you.

MAKES 2 SERVINGS
(ONE 6-INCH CASSEROLE)

3 (6-inch) corn tortillas

½ (15.5-ounce) can black or pinto beans, rinsed and drained

⅓ cup Mexican salsa

½ cup fresh or frozen corn

4 ounces (about 1 cup) shredded Monterey Jack cheese or cheese substitute

4 tablespoons chopped fresh cilantro, divided

Garnishes: sour cream or sour cream alternative, chopped fresh avocado, sliced green onion, and/ or black olives

1. Preheat the oven to 425°F. Generously grease a 6-inch round cake pan (I use a glass pie pan). Place a tortilla on the bottom of the pan. Top with one-third of the beans, one-third of the salsa, one-third of the corn, and one-third of the cheese. Repeat twice more with the remaining tortillas, beans, salsa, and corn and ending with the cheese. Sprinkle with 2 tablespoons of the cilantro. Cover tightly with aluminum foil (or a lid).

2. Bake the casserole, covered, for 20 minutes. Remove the foil and bake until heated through and the cheese is melted and bubbling, about 5 more minutes. Cut in half and serve immediately. Garnish with the 2 tablespoons remaining cilantro and your chosen garnishes.

LEFTOVER BEANS Use the second half of the can of beans in Chilaquiles (page 50).

MAKE-AHEAD LAYERED BEAN-TORTILLA CASSEROLE
Assemble the casserole through Step 1. Cover tightly with foil and refrigerate overnight or all day. Proceed with Step 2, baking for 25 minutes rather than 20 minutes.

Per serving: 435 calories; 24g protein; 19g total fat; 10g fiber; 46g carbohydrates; 50mg cholesterol; 648mg sodium

Sides: Grains, Beans, Legumes & Potatoes

For most of us, preparing side
dishes for small households is easy. It doesn't take any
kitchen math to bake two potatoes . . . or steam two
ears of corn . . . or heat up two servings of green peas
in the microwave.

But for those sides that involve multiple ingredients
or measurements, it gets a little murky. This chapter
includes a diverse collection of what may seem like
unrelated dishes that often round out a meal, but
that also involve measuring multiple ingredients,
which spells confusion if you're not sure about the
proportions.

I am a strong advocate of including gluten-free
grains, legumes, and beans in our diets because they
deliver important nutrients to our bodies—nutrients
we normally ingest in the fortified wheat products
that are no longer available to us. I hope these recipes
will guide you toward increasing your daily intake of
these important foods. Also, check the Main Dishes
chapter for additional dishes that include grains,
beans, and legumes.

Potato dishes are another challenge for those eating
gluten-free because of thickeners and breading;
I've included some here, as well. So dive into this
chapter and enjoy the myriad ways to nourish small
households.

If you're a vegetarian, simply use vegetable broth
instead of chicken broth. If you're a hearty eater, add
mushrooms or protein—such as fish, seafood, pork,
beef, poultry, or tofu.

Soaking time: Overnight
Cooking time: 45 minutes
Preparation time: 10 minutes

Tabbouleh

(V)

Traditionally, tabbouleh is made with bulgur, but my version uses sorghum—an important global cereal grain. Available from Bob's Red Mill and others, sorghum resembles bulgur or wheat berries. It is a hearty, chewy solution to meeting our daily goal of 2 to 3 servings of whole grains, but it does take a long time to cook and needs to soak overnight.

MAKES 2 SERVINGS

Sorghum

⅓ cup uncooked whole grain sorghum, soaked overnight in water to cover

⅔ cup water

⅛ teaspoon salt

Dressing

2 tablespoons fresh lemon juice

2 tablespoons extra-virgin olive oil

1 tablespoon balsamic vinegar

1 tablespoon agave nectar or honey

¼ teaspoon salt

1/16 teaspoon (pinch) white pepper

Add-Ins

2 tablespoons shelled raw pumpkin seeds or pine nuts

3 inches English or hothouse cucumber (unpeeled), chopped

1 green onion, chopped

6 grape or cherry tomatoes, halved

2 tablespoons cooked edamame or snow peas

2 tablespoons chopped fresh parsley, plus extra for garnish

2 tablespoons chopped fresh mint

Handful of mixed greens or spinach, for serving

1. Drain the soaked sorghum and discard the water. In a heavy medium saucepan, combine the sorghum, water, and salt. Bring to a boil. Cover, reduce the heat, and simmer for 40 to 45 minutes, or until tender. Transfer to a strainer, rinse with cold water, and drain well. Set aside.

2. Make the dressing: In a screw-top jar, combine all the ingredients and shake until thoroughly blended and creamy. Set aside.

3. In a large bowl, combine the sorghum and all of the add-ins. Toss with as much of the dressing as needed to coat everything thoroughly. Let stand for 20 minutes before serving.

4. Arrange the mixed greens on a serving platter, top with the tabbouleh, garnish with parsley, and serve.

Exploring Other Ingredients: Tabbouleh is quite versatile. In place of the edamame, use other green vegetables such as steamed green beans or broccoli. To make the tabbouleh a main dish, top with a protein such as cooked seasoned shrimp, chopped chicken, or even salmon.

Per serving: 355 calories; 10g protein; 18g total fat; 8g fiber; 45g carbohydrates; 0mg cholesterol; 290mg sodium

Wild Rice Salad

Wild rice isn't really rice. It is the seed of a grass but still counts toward your daily intake of whole grains. It's hearty and chewy, and its dark color is especially attractive against green and orange fruits and vegetables, like the apricots and snow peas in this salad. The citrusy dressing melds the flavors together nicely. Use vegetable broth to make it vegetarian. Serve with grilled salmon on top to make it a meal.

MAKES 2 SERVINGS
(¾ CUP EACH)

1½ cups gluten-free low-sodium chicken or vegetable broth

½ cup wild rice, rinsed 3 times and drained

¼ teaspoon salt

½ cup fresh snow peas, halved

¼ cup diced dried apricots, or 1 (4-ounce) container mandarin oranges, drained

2 tablespoons chopped toasted pecans

1 tablespoon chopped fresh parsley, plus extra for garnish

1 green onion, chopped

Dressing

1 teaspoon orange zest

2 tablespoons fresh orange juice

1 tablespoon sherry vinegar

1 small garlic clove, minced

⅛ teaspoon (dash) salt

1/16 teaspoon (pinch) freshly ground black pepper

½ teaspoon extra-virgin olive oil

1. In a medium saucepan, bring the broth to a boil over high heat. Add the wild rice and salt. Return to a boil, reduce the heat to low, and simmer, covered, until tender, about 45 minutes. Drain any remaining liquid and transfer the wild rice to a medium bowl.

2. Meanwhile, bring a small pan of water to a boil. Add the snow peas and cook 1 minute, then drain and immerse in cold water to stop the cooking. Add the snow peas to the bowl with the wild rice; add the apricots, pecans, parsley, and green onion.

3. Make the dressing: In a separate small bowl, whisk together the orange zest and juice, vinegar, garlic, salt, and pepper until well blended. Whisk in the oil until slightly thickened.

4. Drizzle the dressing over the salad and toss to coat well. Serve at room temperature, garnished with parsley.

MAKE-AHEAD WILD RICE SALAD You can make this salad several hours before it is served. Simply chill the salad for up to 4 hours. Let it stand at room temperature for 20 minutes, and then serve.

Per serving: 300 calories; 16g protein; 7g total fat; 5g fiber; 47g carbohydrates; 0mg cholesterol; 796mg sodium

Risotto

This is a streamlined risotto, without the constant stirring usually needed, but with some unusual techniques to assure its creaminess. Use vegetable broth to make it vegetarian. To make the dish heartier, add sautéed chopped mushrooms, your favorite vegetables, or small shrimp.

MAKES 2 SERVINGS
(¾ CUP EACH)

1½ cups gluten-free low-sodium chicken or vegetable broth

¼ cup dry white wine or additional broth

⅓ cup Arborio rice

1 teaspoon olive oil

1 tablespoon minced shallot or yellow onion

1 small garlic clove, minced

¼ cup (1 ounce) grated Parmesan cheese or soy Parmesan

1 tablespoon unsalted butter or buttery spread

2 tablespoons heavy cream or half-and-half (optional)

1 tablespoon lemon juice (optional)

Salt and freshly ground black pepper, to taste

1 tablespoon chopped fresh parsley, for garnish

1. Combine the broth and wine in a medium bowl. Add the rice and soak for 30 seconds, stirring with a spoon to agitate the rice and release its starches. Drain the rice through a sieve into a 2-cup measuring cup and reserve the broth (it contains starches that make the risotto creamy).

2. In a heavy 2-quart saucepan, heat the oil over medium heat. Add the drained rice and toast, stirring constantly, just until it starts to smell nutty, about 2 minutes. Add the shallot and garlic. Whisk the broth mixture to distribute the starches and add all but ¼ cup to the saucepan. Stir thoroughly. Cover and cook over low heat for 15 minutes—with a quick stir halfway through—until the rice is tender.

3. Whisk the remaining ¼ cup broth mixture again and add to the risotto, along with the Parmesan, butter, and cream and lemon juice (if using). Stir together. If the risotto is too stiff, add a little hot water to loosen the risotto to your preferred consistency. Taste and add salt and pepper, if desired. Serve, garnished with parsley.

Per serving: 345 calories; 15g protein; 17g total fat; 1g fiber; 29g carbohydrates; 44mg cholesterol; 590mg sodium

Corn Pudding (Spoon Bread)

This comforting side dish is great anytime you want something homestyle and creamy. Growing up, we made corn pudding with fresh sweet corn from our Nebraska garden—which yields the creamiest results—but frozen or canned corn also works too.

MAKES 2 SERVINGS

½ cup thawed frozen corn kernels (5 ounces), or kernels cut from 1 medium ear fresh corn

1 large egg, at room temperature

⅓ cup milk of choice (the richer the better)

1 tablespoon sugar

1 tablespoon unsalted butter or buttery spread, melted

1½ teaspoons Carol's Gluten-Free Flour Blend (page 24) or sweet rice flour

½ teaspoon baking powder

¼ teaspoon salt

⅛ teaspoon (dash) paprika, for garnish

1. Preheat the oven to 350°F. Generously grease two 3¼x1¾-inch (4-ounce) ramekins.

2. In a small bowl, whisk together the corn, egg, milk, sugar, butter, flour blend, baking powder, and salt until well blended (or blend with an electric mixer on low speed). Divide the batter between the ramekins.

3. Bake until the edges start to brown and the centers are just set, 25 to 30 minutes. Cool 5 minutes on a wire rack and then serve hot, garnished with paprika.

Per serving: 170 calories; 5g protein; 9g total fat; 1g fiber; 19g carbohydrates; 111mg cholesterol; 439mg sodium

Easy Microwave Polenta

Okay, so this isn't a multi-ingredient recipe. Nonetheless, I love polenta and look for ways to serve the lovely yellow dish whenever I can. However, I dislike the traditional 20 to 30 minutes needed to cook and stir the polenta, or the splattered cooktop. I instead make mine in the microwave, shaving the cooking time down to about 6 (untended) minutes, without splatters—which frees me to prepare the rest of the meal.

MAKES 2 SERVINGS
(½ CUP EACH)

1½ cups cold water

⅓ cup Bob's Red Mill gluten-free yellow corn grits/polenta

1 teaspoon unsalted butter or buttery spread

2 tablespoons grated Parmesan cheese or soy Parmesan (optional)

¼ teaspoon salt, or to taste

1. Combine all the ingredients in a microwave-safe bowl. Lay a sheet of wax paper over the bowl and cook in the microwave oven on High in two 3-minute increments, whisking between each increment, to reach the desired consistency. (Your microwave might require slightly more or less time.)

2. Serve immediately; polenta gels and firms up as it cools.

AVOIDING BOIL-OVERS Use a large enough container to avoid boil-overs. I use a 4-cup Pyrex measuring cup, which allows plenty of room for boiling within the container.

Per serving: 205 calories; 6g protein; 4g total fat; 5g fiber; 36g carbohydrates; 9mg cholesterol; 384mg sodium

Warm Lentil Salad

In addition to being a great side dish, you can serve these warm lentils under a steak, salmon, or pork chops—as chefs do in upscale restaurants. The savory juices of the meat trickle down into the lentils, adding further seasoning. This is one of my favorite cold-weather dishes because it is hearty, filling, and flavorful.

MAKES 2 SERVINGS
(ABOUT ½ CUP EACH)

½ cup uncooked brown lentils

1 cup gluten-free low-sodium chicken or vegetable broth

1 garlic clove, minced

1 teaspoon dried minced onion

1 teaspoon herbes de Provence or fines herbes

¼ teaspoon salt

2 tablespoons finely diced red bell pepper

1 teaspoon chopped fresh parsley

1 tablespoon extra-virgin olive oil

1 teaspoon sherry or champagne vinegar

Salt and freshly ground pepper, to taste

1. In a medium pan, combine the lentils, broth, garlic, dried onion, herbes de Provence, and salt. Bring to a boil over medium heat. Reduce the heat to low, cover, and simmer for 30 minutes, until the lentils are soft. Drain any excess broth.

2. Stir in the bell pepper, parsley, oil, and vinegar and heat to serving temperature. Season to taste with salt and black pepper. Serve warm.

Per serving: 255 calories; 19g protein; 7g total fat; 15g fiber; 30g carbohydrates; 0mg cholesterol; 531mg sodium

Hash Brown Casserole (V)

This homey dish, which often shows up at Sunday dinners, can be dressed up with peas, corn, or edamame. Or, for a heartier, non-vegetarian dish, add diced ham or Canadian bacon.

MAKES 2 SERVINGS
(ONE 4x8-INCH PAN)

1½ cups frozen shredded hash browns

½ cup (2 ounces) shredded low-fat cheddar cheese or cheese alternative

½ cup low-fat sour cream or sour cream alternative

2 tablespoons milk of choice

2 tablespoons grated Parmesan cheese or soy Parmesan

1 tablespoon dried minced onion

1 small garlic clove, minced

¼ teaspoon salt

¼ teaspoon freshly ground black pepper

1/16 teaspoon (pinch) grated fresh nutmeg (optional)

¼ cup gluten-free bread crumbs (to make your own, see page 127)

1. Place a rack in the middle of the oven. Preheat the oven to 350°F. Generously grease a 4x8-inch nonstick loaf pan.

2. In a medium bowl, toss together all the ingredients except the bread crumbs. Stir with a spatula until thoroughly blended. Spread evenly in the pan. Sprinkle with the bread crumbs and cover tightly with aluminum foil.

3. Bake for 20 to 25 minutes. Remove the foil and bake until the casserole is bubbly around the edges and the bread crumbs are browned, about another 10 minutes. Serve hot.

KEEPING BREAD CRUMBS ON HAND Always keep your gluten-free bread crumbs in the freezer so they won't go stale. And having them on hand means you can instantly measure small quantities, like the ¼ cup in this recipe.

Per serving: 290 calories; 16g protein; 7g total fat; 3g fiber; 44g carbohydrates; 15mg cholesterol; 706mg sodium

Roasted Potato Wedges

These are a favorite at our house and often the go-to dish for winter meals. I love thyme, but you can use any of the other herb suggestions. If you don't have fresh herbs, use half as much of the dried version. I have also used flavored salts such as smoked salt—which is delicious with the wedges.

MAKES 2 SERVINGS

1 medium baking or russet potato (about ½ pound), rinsed and patted dry

1 tablespoon extra-virgin olive oil

1 teaspoon minced fresh herbs (thyme, dill, marjoram, parsley, or rosemary)

⅛ teaspoon (dash) garlic powder (optional)

¼ teaspoon salt, or to taste

¼ teaspoon freshly ground black pepper, or to taste

1. Preheat the oven to 400°F. Line a 9x13-inch rimmed baking sheet with parchment paper. (Or use aluminum foil and coat it with cooking spray.)

2. Halve the potato lengthwise. Then cut each half into three lengthwise wedges for a total of 6 wedges. In a large bowl, toss the wedges with the oil, herbs, garlic powder, salt, and pepper until thoroughly coated. Arrange the wedges on the baking sheet, with one of the cut sides down.

3. Roast for 20 minutes. Turn each wedge to the other cut side and roast another 15 minutes, until the wedges are lightly browned and crisp on the outside, but tender on the inside. Sprinkle with more salt and pepper, if desired.

Per serving: 135 calories; 2g protein; 7g total fat; 2g fiber; 17g carbohydrates; 0mg cholesterol; 272mg sodium

Potato Pancakes (Latkes)

Potato pancakes, also known as latkes, are simple to make and perfect with roasted meats. I especially love to top them with applesauce and sour cream and serve alongside smoked pork chops. (For me, my mother's version of store-bought, canned sauerkraut—drained, rinsed, and tossed with sugar and caraway seeds—completes the meal.) Work quickly with grated potatoes since they discolor when exposed to air.

MAKES 2 SERVINGS
(2 PANCAKES EACH)

2 tablespoons cornstarch

½ teaspoon baking powder

¼ teaspoon onion powder

¼ teaspoon salt

1/16 teaspoon (pinch) freshly ground black pepper

1 cup grated peeled russet potatoes (about ½ pound)

1 egg white, well beaten

1 tablespoon canola oil

Optional garnishes and go-withs: paprika, chopped chives or green onions, sour cream, applesauce

1. In a medium bowl, whisk together the cornstarch, baking powder, onion powder, salt, and pepper. Add the grated potatoes and egg white and stir to combine thoroughly.

2. In a 10-inch nonstick skillet, heat the oil over medium heat. Use a ¼-cup metal measuring cup to drop four mounds of batter in the skillet. Flatten each mound slightly with a spatula, if necessary.

3. Fry the pancakes until lightly browned, about 5 minutes on each side. Serve immediately, with garnishes if desired.

LEFTOVER EGG YOLK Save the unused egg yolk and toss it into the other eggs for the Herb Frittata (page 46) or use it in scrambled eggs.

Per serving: 160 calories; 3g protein; 7g total fat; 1g fiber; 22g carbohydrates; 0mg cholesterol; 421mg sodium

Fried Mashed Potato Patties

Here's a great way to use leftover mashed potatoes. We have them about once a week at our house. In fact, I often make extra mashed potatoes just so we can have these patties at a later meal. For variety, stir thinly sliced green onions or chopped fresh herbs into the mashed potato mixture before frying.

MAKES 2 SERVINGS
(2 SMALL PATTIES EACH)

1 tablespoon canola oil

1 tablespoon unsalted butter or buttery spread (or additional canola oil)

1 cup chilled leftover mashed potatoes, from 1 large (1-pound) russet potato

¼ teaspoon salt (optional, depending on saltiness of the mashed potatoes)

⅛ teaspoon (dash) freshly ground black pepper (optional)

In a 10-inch nonstick skillet, heat the oil and butter over medium heat. For each patty, add ¼ cup of the mashed potato mixture to the hot skillet and press lightly with a spatula to flatten slightly. Cook the patties until they form a golden crust on the bottom, 3 to 5 minutes, depending on the potatoes. (Peek underneath using a spatula before turning them over.) Turn and cook the other sides until golden brown, about 3 minutes. Serve hot, seasoned with salt and pepper, if desired.

Per serving: 225 calories; 2g protein; 17g total fat; 2g fiber; 18g carbohydrates; 18mg cholesterol; 513mg sodium

Citrusy Brussels Sprouts with Pancetta

I have been eating a dish similar to this in restaurants for many years. It is perfect for small households because you can buy as many or as few Brussels sprouts as you like from the vegetable bin. Pancetta is Italian bacon and lends a crispy saltiness that contrasts nicely with the sweetness from the orange marmalade. For ease, buy pre-diced pancetta in packages at the deli and freeze the remainder for another day. Or, use a slice of browned, crumbled bacon instead. My family likes this dish so much that it has been elevated to Thanksgiving/Christmas dinner status.

MAKES 2 SERVINGS

1 tablespoon (about ¼ ounce) diced pancetta

1 teaspoon olive oil

2 cups small Brussels sprouts, trimmed and halved (about 8 ounces)

$\frac{1}{16}$ teaspoon (pinch) salt

$\frac{1}{16}$ teaspoon (pinch) freshly ground black pepper

1 tablespoon orange juice

1 tablespoon orange marmalade (or your favorite citrus-based preserve)

½ teaspoon balsamic vinegar

1. Heat a 10-inch skillet over medium heat. Add the pancetta and cook, stirring constantly, until crispy, 1 to 2 minutes. Transfer the pancetta to a plate, leaving any remaining fat in the skillet.

2. Add the olive oil to the skillet. Arrange the Brussels sprouts, cut sides down, in a single layer in the skillet and sprinkle with the salt and pepper. Cover and cook over medium heat until the sprouts are tender and lightly browned, 5 to 7 minutes, depending on size and thickness.

3. Remove the pan from the heat and stir in the orange juice, marmalade, balsamic vinegar, and pancetta. Toss until everything is coated with the glaze and serve immediately.

Per serving: 95 calories; 4g protein; 3g total fat; 4g fiber; 15g carbohydrates; 2mg cholesterol; 190mg sodium

Preparation time: 10 minutes
Cooking time: 15 minutes
Chilling time: 2 hours

⚜ Potato Salad ⓥ

It isn't summer without potato salad, but the conundrum is how much of its many ingredients to use for two servings. My version eliminates the guesswork. I prefer to leave the potatoes unpeeled for the added nutrients, but peel them if you wish. For best results, add the potatoes to the dressing while they're hot so they absorb more flavor. And, if you have it, a teaspoon of chopped fresh dill makes this delightful. This makes a "dry" potato salad; for a wetter version, increase the mayonnaise to taste.

MAKES 2 SERVINGS
(ABOUT ¾ CUP EACH)

2 tablespoons mayonnaise or Miracle Whip salad dressing

2 teaspoons sweet pickle relish

1 teaspoon cider vinegar

1 teaspoon Dijon mustard

¼ teaspoon granulated sugar

¼ teaspoon celery salt or table salt

$\frac{1}{16}$ teaspoon (pinch) celery seed

$\frac{1}{16}$ teaspoon (pinch) freshly ground black pepper

1 (6-ounce) Russet potato, diced (about 1 cup)

1 large egg, hard-boiled, peeled, and chopped

2 tablespoons finely diced celery

2 tablespoons finely diced green onion, shallot, or fresh chives

Salt and freshly ground pepper, to taste

1 teaspoon chopped fresh parsley, or 1½ teaspoons dried, for garnish

¼ teaspoon paprika, for garnish

1. In a medium bowl, make the dressing by whisking together the mayonnaise, relish, vinegar, mustard, sugar, celery salt, celery seed, and the $\frac{1}{16}$ teaspoon (pinch) black pepper until thoroughly blended. Set aside.

2. Cook the potato in boiling salted water for 15 minutes, or until tender. Drain thoroughly and add to the bowl, tossing until the potatoes are thoroughly coated with dressing. Add the egg, celery, and onion to the bowl. Stir with a spatula until all of the ingredients are thoroughly coated with the dressing. Taste and add salt and additional pepper, if desired. Transfer the potato salad to a serving bowl, cover, and chill for 2 hours or up to 6 hours.

3. To serve, let stand at room temperature for 15 minutes. Sprinkle with parsley and paprika and serve.

Per serving: 190 calories; 5g protein; 10g total fat; 2g fiber; 23g carbohydrates; 98mg cholesterol; 552mg sodium

Breads

Bread baking is one of the joys

of my life. Yet, of all the gluten-free recipes we prepare at home, bread recipes may be the hardest to adapt to small sizes. There are so many ingredients to consider and—as gluten-free bakers inevitably learn—it can involve complicated kitchen math. Why? Because not all ingredients scale down in the same proportions—especially in bread—so you can't just halve the ingredients in a recipe for four to serve two. For example, sometimes you need more salt, sometimes less. Yeast doesn't scale down proportionally, either. But don't worry, I tested and figured it out so all you have to do is follow my easy directions and you can have just enough bread for your household.

Given the growing interest in the Paleo diet (which eliminates grains of all kinds) and an increasing number of gluten-free people who don't digest any grains properly, I have included two grain-free muffins in this chapter. Even if you're not grain-free, go ahead and try them; they will provide variety to your gluten-free baking.

Basic Muffins

Ⓥ

If you make this basic muffin without any variations, use butter or buttery spread for a delightful buttery flavor. But if you're making one of the flavorful variations below, you can use oil because the fruit and grated citrus zest add lots of flavor. You can even use melted coconut oil (one of my favorites) instead of butter.

MAKES 4 MUFFINS

½ cup Carol's Gluten-Free Flour Blend (page 24)

¼ cup granulated sugar, plus extra for sprinkling

½ teaspoon baking powder

½ teaspoon xanthan gum

⅛ teaspoon (dash) salt

¹⁄₁₆ teaspoon (pinch) baking soda

¼ cup milk of choice, at room temperature

2 tablespoons unsalted butter or buttery spread, melted and cooled, or canola oil

1 large egg, at room temperature

½ teaspoon pure vanilla extract

1. Place a rack in the lower third of the oven. Preheat the oven to 375°F. Generously grease 4 cups of a standard 6-cup nonstick muffin pan or line with paper liners.

2. In a medium mixing bowl, whisk together the flour blend, sugar, baking powder, xanthan gum, salt, and baking soda until well blended. With the electric mixer on low speed, beat in the milk, butter, egg, and vanilla just until blended. Divide the batter evenly among the muffin cups (for perfectly proportioned muffins, use a 1½-inch metal spring-action ice cream scoop to portion the batter). Sprinkle the tops with a little sugar.

3. Bake until the muffin tops are lightly browned, 20 to 25 minutes. Cool the muffins in the pan on a wire rack for 10 minutes, then remove the muffins from the pan and cool on the rack for another 10 minutes. Serve slightly warm.

Blueberry-Lemon Muffins: Gently stir ¼ cup fresh blueberries and 1 teaspoon grated lemon zest into the batter. Bake as directed.

Per muffin: 200 calories; 3g protein; 7g total fat; 1g fiber; 30g carbohydrates; 63mg cholesterol; 231mg sodium

Cranberry-Orange Muffins: Gently stir ¼ cup dried cranberries and 1 teaspoon grated orange zest into the batter. Bake as directed.

Per muffin: 195 calories; 2g protein; 7g total fat; 1g fiber; 29g carbohydrates; 63mg cholesterol; 230mg sodium

Lemon–Poppy Seed Muffins: Gently stir 1 teaspoon poppy seeds and 1 teaspoon grated lemon zest into the batter. Bake as directed.

Per muffin: 195 calories; 3g protein; 8g total fat; 1g fiber; 29g carbohydrates; 63mg cholesterol; 230mg sodium

Raspberry-Almond Muffins: Use almond extract instead of vanilla and add ½ teaspoon ground cinnamon with the salt. Gently stir ¼ cup fresh raspberries into the batter. Bake as directed.

Per muffin: 195 calories; 3g protein; 7g total fat; 1g fiber; 30g carbohydrates; 63mg cholesterol; 219mg sodium

Per muffin: 195 calories; 2g protein; 7g total fat; 1g fiber; 29g carbohydrates; 63mg cholesterol; 230mg sodium

Grain-Free Flax Muffins with Coconut Streusel ⓥ

Flax is a very healthy, high-fiber seed, and the meal ground from it makes an excellent grain-free flour. This muffin travels well because its density resists crumbling. As my mother used to say, "It will stick to your ribs!"

MAKES 4 MUFFINS

½ cup ground flaxseed meal

¼ cup almond meal/flour

1 teaspoon baking powder

½ teaspoon xanthan gum

¼ teaspoon salt

⅛ teaspoon (dash) baking soda

3 tablespoons honey, warmed slightly if stiff

2 tablespoons canola oil

1 large egg, at room temperature

½ teaspoon pure vanilla extract

¼ cup sweetened shredded coconut

2 tablespoons dried cranberries

Coconut-Streusel Topping

1 tablespoon granulated sugar

2 teaspoons Carol's Gluten-Free Flour Blend (page 24)

⅛ teaspoon (dash) canola oil, or more if needed

1 teaspoon sweetened shredded coconut

1. Preheat the oven to 350°F. Generously grease 4 cups of a standard 6-cup nonstick muffin pan or line with paper liners.

2. In a medium bowl, whisk together the flaxseed meal, almond meal/flour, baking powder, xanthan gum, salt, and baking soda until well blended. In a small measuring cup, whisk together the honey, oil, egg, and vanilla until well blended. Gradually whisk the egg mixture into the flax mixture until just blended. Stir in the coconut and cranberries. Divide the batter evenly among the muffin cups (for uniformly sized muffins, use a 1½-inch metal spring-action ice cream scoop to portion the batter).

3. Make the streusel: In a small ramekin, whisk together the sugar and flour blend with a fork until well blended. Mix in the oil with the fork until the mixture resembles wet sand. (If needed, add more oil, a drop at a time, to reach this consistency.) Stir in the coconut.

4. Sprinkle the streusel evenly over the muffin batter. Bake until the tops are brown and the muffins are firm, 20 to 25 minutes. Cool the muffins on a wire rack in the pan for 15 minutes, and then remove the muffins from the pan. Serve slightly warm.

Per muffin: 310 calories; 9g protein; 21g total fat; 6g fiber; 24g carbohydrates; 47mg cholesterol; 300mg sodium

Grain-Free Banana-Raisin Muffins

Ⓥ

This not-too-sweet, almond flour–based muffin is appropriate for those who avoid all grains. It makes a dense, moist muffin and travels well. If you like, experiment with alternative sweeteners in place of the brown sugar. Try maple sugar, coconut sugar, or date sugar; each lends its own distinct flavor. You can also replace the raisins with dried cranberries, blueberries, or cherries . . . or the same amount of mini chocolate chips, since it's okay to have chocolate for breakfast at my house!

MAKES 6 MUFFINS

¾ cup almond meal/flour

1 teaspoon cinnamon

½ teaspoon baking soda

½ teaspoon xanthan gum

¼ teaspoon salt

1 large egg, at room temperature

½ cup mashed ripe banana, about 1 medium banana

¼ cup packed brown sugar

2 tablespoons canola oil or grapeseed oil, or coconut oil (melted and slightly cooled)

½ teaspoon pure vanilla extract

½ cup raisins or chopped dried plums, or pitted and finely chopped dates

1. Place a rack in the middle of the oven. Preheat the oven to 325°F. Generously grease the cups of a 6-cup standard muffin pan or line with paper liners.

2. In a medium bowl, whisk together the almond meal/flour, cinnamon, baking soda, xanthan gum, and salt until well blended. In a small bowl, beat the egg, banana, brown sugar, oil, and vanilla together with a fork or whisk until smooth. Stir the banana mixture into the almond meal/flour mixture until well blended. Stir in the raisins. Divide the batter evenly among the muffin cups (for perfectly proportioned muffins, use a 1½-inch metal spring-action ice cream scoop to portion the batter).

3. Bake for 30 to 35 minutes, until a toothpick inserted into the center of a muffin comes out clean. Cool the muffins in the pan on a wire rack for 15 minutes and then remove the muffins from the pan. Serve slightly warm.

Per muffin: 210 calories, 8g protein; 9g total fat; 2g fiber; 29g carbohydrates; 31mg cholesterol; 224mg sodium

Oatmeal-Raisin Muffins in a Mug

Ⓥ

To save time in the morning, whisk together the dry ingredients and wet ingredients in separate bowls the night before and refrigerate the wet ingredients. The next morning, whisk everything together, add the raisins, and bake in the coffee cups. You just eat the muffin with a spoon right out of the cup.

MAKES 2 MUFFINS

¼ cup gluten-free quick-cooking oats*

¼ cup cornstarch

¼ teaspoon baking powder

⅛ teaspoon (dash) xanthan gum

¹⁄₁₆ teaspoon (pinch) baking soda

¹⁄₁₆ teaspoon (pinch) cinnamon

¹⁄₁₆ teaspoon (pinch) salt

1 large egg, at room temperature

2 tablespoons molasses (not blackstrap)

1 tablespoon canola oil

1 teaspoon grated orange zest

2 tablespoons raisins

1. Generously grease 2 coffee cups. I use 6-ounce cups, 2¼ inches high and 3½ inches in diameter at the top. The size and diameter of the coffee cup determines how high the muffin rises and whether it spills over the rim as it bakes. The muffin might spill over the edge if you use a smaller cup.

2. In a small bowl, whisk together the oats, cornstarch, baking powder, xanthan gum, baking soda, cinnamon, and salt until thoroughly blended. Whisk in the egg, molasses, oil, orange zest, and raisins until the batter thickens slightly. Divide the batter evenly between the cups. Let stand 5 minutes.

3. Microwave on High for 60 to 70 seconds, until the tops no longer look wet. Let stand for a minute to cool slightly. Eat with a spoon right out of the cup.

NO CRUNCHY TOPS? Microwave muffins don't brown like oven-baked muffins, which means there are no crispy, browned crusts on the top or sides. If you like crunchy crusts, you might want to stick to oven-based recipes.

Check with your physician to make sure gluten-free oats are right for your diet.

Per muffin: 275 calories; 5g protein; 10g total fat; 2g fiber; 44g carbohydrates; 94mg cholesterol; 211mg sodium

Banana Bread ⓥ

The smell of banana bread baking reminds me of home and family. It is certainly one of America's favorite comfort foods, so it had to be in this book. I've been making it since I was a young bride, but always in the huge 5x9-inch loaves. Here's a cute little loaf, just for two.

MAKES 4 SLICES
(ONE 3¼x5¾-INCH LOAF)

1 large egg, at room temperature

⅓ cup mashed overripe banana (about 1 small)

2 tablespoons canola oil

½ cup Carol's Gluten-Free Flour Blend (page 24)

⅓ cup granulated sugar

½ teaspoon baking powder

½ teaspoon xanthan gum

½ teaspoon cinnamon

¹⁄₁₆ teaspoon (pinch) baking soda

¼ teaspoon salt

2 tablespoons chopped walnuts or pecans

1. Place a rack in the lower third of the oven. Preheat the oven to 350°F. Generously grease a 3¼x5¾-inch nonstick loaf pan (gray, not black).

2. In a medium bowl or measuring cup, whisk together the egg, banana, and oil until smooth. In a small bowl, whisk together the flour blend, sugar, baking powder, xanthan gum, cinnamon, baking soda, and salt until well blended. With an electric mixer on low speed, gradually beat the flour mixture into the egg mixture just until blended. Stir the walnuts into the batter. Spread the batter evenly in the pan.

3. Bake until the top is nicely browned and a toothpick inserted into the center comes out clean, 35 to 40 minutes. Cool the bread in the pan on a wire rack for 10 minutes, then remove the bread and cool on the rack for another 10 minutes. Use a serrated knife or an electric knife to cut into 4 slices. Serve slightly warm or at room temperature.

Per slice: 250 calories; 3g protein; 10g total fat; 1g fiber; 36g carbohydrates; 47mg cholesterol; 240mg sodium

Scones

Scones are popular in coffeehouses, but it's hard to find gluten-free versions. So, make your own! They are really quite simple. Once the dough is mixed, work quickly to shape it and get it into the oven so the leavenings can get to work. You can serve scones with anything you like, but—if you ask the English—the traditional options are strawberry jam and clotted cream.

MAKES 4 SCONES

⅔ cup Carol's Gluten-Free Flour Blend (page 24)

¼ cup tapioca flour

2 tablespoons granulated sugar, plus 1 teaspoon for sprinkling

¾ teaspoon cream of tartar

½ teaspoon xanthan gum

¼ teaspoon baking soda

¼ teaspoon salt

3 tablespoons cold unsalted butter, buttery spread, or coconut oil, cut into ½-inch pieces

1 large egg, at room temperature, beaten to a foam

1 tablespoon milk of choice

½ teaspoon pure vanilla extract

¼ cup currants

1. Place a rack in the lower third of the oven. Preheat the oven to 375°F. Grease a 9x13-inch rimmed baking sheet (not nonstick) or line with parchment paper.

2. In a food processor, blend the flour blend, tapioca, sugar, cream of tartar, xanthan gum, baking soda, salt, and butter until crumbly. Reserve 1 tablespoon of the beaten egg for brushing on the scone tops. Add the remaining egg, the milk, and vanilla to the dry ingredients and pulse just until blended. Add the currants and pulse twice to incorporate. (Or, in a medium bowl, mix the dry ingredients and butter with an electric mixer on low speed until the mixture is crumbly. Beat in the egg, milk, and vanilla until blended, then stir in the currants.) The dough will seem too soft to hold its shape, but that's okay.

continued~

3. Transfer the dough to the baking sheet and pat with a wet spatula into a smooth 5-inch circle that is ¾ inch thick. Make sure the dough is the same thickness across the entire circle, rather than tapering at the outer edges; thinner edges brown too quickly and can burn. Whisk the reserved 1 tablespoon egg with ½ teaspoon water and use a pastry brush to brush the mixture over the top and sides of the circle. Sprinkle with the remaining 1 teaspoon sugar.

4. Bake until the top is browned and crisp, 15 to 20 minutes. Remove the baking sheet from the oven, but leave the oven on. With a serrated knife, cut the dough into 4 quarters and pull the wedges about ½ inch away from the center so the innermost edges are exposed to the heat and can crisp up a little. Return the sheet to the oven and bake another 5 to 7 minutes, or until the edges look dry and firm. Cool the scones on the pan for 10 minutes, then serve slightly warm.

SCONES WITH FROSTING DRIZZLE Scones are delicious on their own, but a drizzle of frosting takes them to the next level. Make a batch of Vanilla–Powdered Sugar Frosting (page 227). Thin the frosting with a little water, 1 teaspoon at a time, until the frosting easily falls off a spoon. With a tablespoon of frosting at a time, use back-and-forth motions to drizzle the frosting on each cooled scone. Serve immediately.

Per scone: 330 calories; 3g protein; 10g total fat; 2g fiber; 57g carbohydrates; 70mg cholesterol; 353mg sodium

Buttermilk Biscuits Ⓥ

I grew up on biscuits, so I know they are best piping hot, straight from the oven. And they don't have to be round—square shapes are easier and taste the same . . . trust me on this! These biscuits rise better the less they are handled, so be gentle with them.

MAKES 4 BISCUITS

½ cup Carol's Gluten-Free Flour Blend (page 24)

¼ cup cornstarch or potato starch, plus more for dusting

1½ teaspoons granulated sugar

1 teaspoon baking powder

½ teaspoon xanthan gum

¼ teaspoon salt

⅛ teaspoon (dash) baking soda

⅓ cup buttermilk or plain kefir (or combine ⅓ cup milk of choice and ½ teaspoon vinegar)

2 tablespoons unsalted butter, buttery spread, or vegetable shortening, melted and slightly cooled, plus extra for brushing

1. Place a rack in the lower third of the oven. Preheat the oven to 375°F. Grease a 9x13-inch rimmed baking sheet (not nonstick) or line with parchment paper. Dust the surface lightly with cornstarch.

2. In a medium bowl, whisk together the flour blend, cornstarch, sugar, baking powder, xanthan gum, salt, and baking soda until well blended. Stir the buttermilk and butter together and add to the bowl. Mix with an electric mixer on low speed until a dough forms, scraping down the bowl with a spatula as needed. The dough will be very soft and sticky.

3. Place the dough on the baking sheet and lightly dust with cornstarch to prevent your hands from sticking. Gently pat the dough to a 4-inch square that is ¾ inch thick. Brush the top with the melted butter. With a sharp knife, cut the dough into four squares and use a thin spatula to carefully arrange them on the baking sheet about 1 inch apart.

4. Bake until the biscuits are lightly browned, 12 to 15 minutes. Serve immediately.

BROWNER TOPS If you love browner tops on your biscuits, brush them with heavy cream rather than butter to encourage more browning.

Per biscuit: 165 calories; 1g protein; 6g total fat; 1g fiber; 25g carbohydrates; 16mg cholesterol; 387mg sodium

Pumpkin Spice Quick Bread

ⓥ

I always salivate when I see the pumpkin bread at coffee shops. It smells so good, but it is never gluten-free! Here is my small-scale version, which contains a lot of spices to produce that terrific flavor and aroma. Your kitchen will smell heavenly! The cute little loaves also make great gifts for your gluten-free friends.

MAKES 4 SLICES
(ONE 3¼x5¾-INCH LOAF)

1 large egg, at room temperature

½ cup canned pure pumpkin (not pumpkin pie filling)

3 tablespoons canola oil

½ cup Carol's Gluten-Free Flour Blend (page 24)

⅓ cup plus 1 tablespoon granulated sugar

1 teaspoon pumpkin pie spice

½ teaspoon baking powder

½ teaspoon xanthan gum

¼ rounded teaspoon salt

1/16 teaspoon (pinch) baking soda

1 tablespoon finely chopped raw pumpkin seeds

1. Place a rack in the lower third of the oven. Preheat the oven to 350°F. Generously grease a 3¼x5¾-inch nonstick loaf pan (gray, not black).

2. In a medium bowl, whisk together the egg, pumpkin, and oil until smooth. In a small bowl, whisk together the flour blend, all the sugar, the pumpkin pie spice, baking powder, xanthan gum, salt, and baking soda until well blended. With an electric mixer on low speed, gradually beat the flour mixture into the egg mixture just until blended. Spread the batter evenly in the pan and sprinkle the pumpkin seeds evenly on top, slightly pressing them into the batter with your fingers.

3. Bake until the top is nicely browned and a toothpick inserted into the center comes out clean, 35 to 40 minutes. Cool the bread in the pan on a wire rack for 10 minutes, then remove the bread and cool on the rack for another 10 minutes. Use a serrated knife or an electric knife to cut into 4 slices, and serve slightly warm or at room temperature.

Per slice: 265 calories; 2g protein; 12g total fat; 2g fiber; 38g carbohydrates; 47mg cholesterol; 241mg sodium

Zucchini Bread

Trust me, this recipe may not be top-of-mind right now, but the next time your garden over-produces or your neighbors unload their zucchini crop on you—well, you will thank me for this recipe. Yet, you will only make as much as you need, which is one cute little loaf. Be sure to wring the grated zucchini very dry in a towel to remove excess moisture. The allspice lends a nice note, so use it if you can.

MAKES 4 SLICES
(ONE 3¼x5¾-INCH LOAF)

½ cup Carol's Gluten-Free Flour Blend (page 24)

⅓ cup granulated sugar

½ teaspoon baking powder

½ teaspoon cinnamon

½ teaspoon xanthan gum

½ teaspoon salt

¼ teaspoon allspice (optional)

¹⁄₁₆ teaspoon (pinch) baking soda

1 large egg, at room temperature

2 tablespoons canola oil

½ teaspoon pure vanilla extract

½ cup grated zucchini (about 1 very small zucchini), wrung dry in a towel

2 tablespoons raisins

2 tablespoons chopped pecans (or your favorite nuts)

1. Place a rack in the lower third of the oven. Preheat the oven to 350°F. Generously grease a 3¼x5¾-inch nonstick loaf pan (gray, not black).

2. In a small bowl, whisk together the flour blend, sugar, baking powder, cinnamon, xanthan gum, salt, allspice (if using), and baking soda until well blended. In a medium mixing bowl, beat the egg with an electric mixer on medium speed until light yellow and frothy, about 30 seconds. Add the oil and vanilla and beat on low speed until well blended. With the mixer on low speed, beat the flour mixture gradually into the egg mixture until the batter is smooth. The batter will be very stiff. Beat in the grated zucchini; the batter will become much softer. With a spatula, stir in the raisins and nuts. Spread the batter evenly in the pan.

3. Bake until the top is nicely browned and a toothpick inserted into the center comes out clean, 35 to 40 minutes. Cool the bread in the pan for 10 minutes on a wire rack. Remove the bread from the pan and cool completely on the rack. Slice with a serrated knife and serve slightly warm.

Per slice: 255 calories; 3g protein; 11g total fat; 2g fiber; 38g carbohydrates; 47mg cholesterol; 385mg sodium

Cheddar Cheese Quick Bread

ⓥ

This savory quick bread complements soups and main-dish salads — a nice way to add a bit of heft to an otherwise light meal. Extra-sharp cheddar produces the most pronounced flavor, but the bread is delicious with mild cheddar as well. Shredded cheese melts right into the bread, while diced cheese produces cheesy pockets.

MAKES 4 SLICES
(ONE 3¼ x 5¾-INCH LOAF)

½ cup Carol's Gluten-Free Flour Blend (page 24)

1 tablespoon granulated sugar

¾ teaspoon baking powder

½ teaspoon xanthan gum

½ teaspoon onion powder

1 large egg, at room temperature

2 tablespoons unsalted butter, buttery spread, or coconut oil, melted and slightly cooled

½ cup (2 ounces) coarsely shredded or diced cheddar cheese or Daiya cheddar-style shreds

2 tablespoons grated Parmesan cheese or soy Parmesan, divided

1. Place a rack in the middle of the oven. Preheat the oven to 375°F. Generously grease a 3¼x5¾-inch nonstick loaf pan (gray, not black).

2. In a small mixing bowl, whisk together the flour blend, sugar, baking powder, xanthan gum, and onion powder until well blended. Add the egg and butter and beat with an electric mixer on low speed until well blended, about 30 seconds. Gently stir in the cheddar and 1 tablespoon of the Parmesan. The dough will be somewhat stiff.

3. Spread the batter evenly in the pan and smooth the top with a wet spatula. Sprinkle the remaining 1 tablespoon Parmesan on top.

4. Bake, rotating the pan halfway through baking, until the top is browned and a toothpick inserted into the center of the loaf comes out clean, 35 to 40 minutes. If necessary, cover with foil after 15 minutes of baking to prevent overbrowning. Cool the bread 10 minutes in the pan on a wire rack. Remove the bread from the pan and cool for 20 minutes on the rack. Serve slightly warm.

Per serving: 370 calories; 13g protein; 18g total fat; 1g fiber; 38g carbohydrates; 134mg cholesterol; 617mg sodium

 Cornbread

(V)

Cornbread is a great accompaniment to soup or stew. My husband and I like to eat one slice with the main dish, then another slice with honey as dessert. I grew up in the Midwest where we like cornbread a little sweeter than they do in the South, so my version is on the sweet side.

MAKES 4 SLICES
(ONE 3¼x5¾-INCH LOAF)

½ cup cornmeal

¼ cup Carol's Gluten-Free Flour Blend (page 24)

2 tablespoons granulated sugar

¾ teaspoon baking powder

½ teaspoon xanthan gum

½ teaspoon salt

¹⁄₁₆ teaspoon (pinch) baking soda

1 large egg, at room temperature

¼ cup water, at room temperature

2 tablespoons canola oil, or coconut oil, melted and slightly cooled

1. Place a rack in the lower third of the oven. Preheat the oven to 350°F. Generously grease a 3¼x5¾-inch nonstick loaf pan (gray, not black).

2. In a medium mixing bowl, whisk together the cornmeal, flour blend, sugar, baking powder, xanthan gum, salt, and baking soda until well blended. With the electric mixer on low speed, beat in the egg, water, and oil until just blended. Increase the speed to medium-low and beat until the batter is slightly thickened, about 30 seconds. The batter will be the consistency of thick cake batter. Spread the batter evenly in the pan.

3. Bake until the top is firm and a toothpick inserted into the center comes out clean, 18 to 20 minutes. Cool the cornbread in the pan on a wire rack for 10 minutes. Serve warm.

Per slice: 200 calories; 3g protein; 8g total fat; 2g fiber; 28g carbohydrates; 47mg cholesterol; 404mg sodium

Preparation time: 10 minutes
Rising time: 30 to 45 minutes
Baking time: 15 to 20 minutes

Focaccia

(V)

Focaccia is a flatbread, similar to pizza. One of the easiest yeast breads you will ever make, this downsized recipe is full of flavor. It makes a 4x8-inch bread that is about 1½ inches thick. Like most gluten-free yeast breads, this one is best when eaten the same day it is baked.

MAKES 8 PIECES
(ONE 4x8-INCH FLATBREAD)

Dough

1 teaspoon active dry yeast

1 teaspoon granulated sugar

⅓ cup warm (110°F) milk of choice

¾ cup Carol's Gluten-Free Flour Blend (page 24)

½ teaspoon xanthan gum

1 teaspoon finely chopped fresh rosemary; or ½ teaspoon dried, crushed in your palm

¼ teaspoon onion powder

⅛ teaspoon (dash) salt

1 large egg, at room temperature

1 tablespoon olive oil, plus more for the pan

1 teaspoon cider vinegar

Topping

2 teaspoons olive oil

½ teaspoon finely chopped fresh rosemary or ¼ teaspoon dried Italian seasoning

⅛ teaspoon (dash) kosher or coarse sea salt

1 tablespoon grated Parmesan cheese or soy Parmesan

1. Make the dough: In a small bowl, dissolve the yeast and sugar in the warm milk. Set aside until foamy, about 5 minutes. Generously coat a 4x8-inch nonstick pan (gray, not black) with olive oil.

2. In a medium mixing bowl, beat the yeast-milk mixture and all of the remaining dough ingredients with an electric mixer on low speed until blended. The dough will be very soft and sticky.

3. With a wet spatula, spread the dough evenly in the pan. Cover with lightly greased aluminum foil and let rise at room temperature (75°F to 85°F) until the dough is doubled in height, 30 to 45 minutes.

4. While the bread rises, preheat the oven to 400°F. Place a rack in the lower third of the oven. Sprinkle the dough with the topping of oil, rosemary, salt, and Parmesan. Bake the focaccia until the top is golden brown, 15 to 20 minutes. Cool the bread in the pan on a wire rack for 10 minutes. Transfer to a cutting board and cut into 8 pieces with an electric or serrated knife. Serve slightly warm.

Per piece: 95 calories; 2g protein; 4g total fat; 1g fiber; 13g carbohydrates; 24mg cholesterol; 97mg sodium

Preparation time: 10 minutes
Rising time: None
Baking time: 12 to 15 minutes

Herbed Flatbread with Dipping Oil

Ⓥ

This flatbread is so thin and supple that you can fold it like a soft taco. I like rosemary, but you can use any herb you wish in the bread. The cold oven method assures that the bread rises slightly, but bakes quickly. The flatbread is best served warm on the same day it is baked. Try different toppings: Arugula is great for a bit of green, but try anything you wish—even pizza toppings.

MAKES 8 PIECES
(ONE 8X12-INCH FLATBREAD)

Dipping Oil

2 tablespoons extra-virgin olive oil

1 tablespoon balsamic vinegar

¼ teaspoon dried oregano

¼ teaspoon dried thyme

Coarse salt and freshly ground pepper, to taste

Dough

1 teaspoon active dry yeast

1 teaspoon granulated sugar

⅓ cup warm (110°F) milk of choice

½ cup Carol's Gluten-Free Flour Blend (page 24)

¼ cup sweet rice flour

½ teaspoon xanthan gum

1 teaspoon chopped fresh rosemary (or basil or thyme); or ½ teaspoon dried, crushed in your palm

¼ teaspoon onion powder

¼ teaspoon salt

1 large egg, at room temperature

1 tablespoon olive oil

½ teaspoon cider vinegar

Topping

Coarse salt

Extra-virgin olive oil (optional)

Grated Parmesan cheese

Arugula (optional)

1. Make the dipping oil: In a small bowl, whisk all the ingredients together until well blended.

2. Make the dough: In a small bowl, dissolve the yeast and sugar in the warm milk. Set aside until foamy, about 5 minutes. Generously grease a 9x13-inch nonstick rimmed baking sheet or cookie sheet (gray, not black).

3. In a medium mixing bowl, whisk together the sweet flour blend, rice flour, xanthan gum, rosemary, onion powder, and salt until well blended. Add the yeast mixture, then add the egg, olive oil, and cider vinegar. Beat with an electric mixer on low speed until blended. The dough will be soft and very sticky.

4. Transfer the dough to the baking sheet and use a wet spatula to smooth it into a very thin layer that measures 8x12 inches, keeping the thickness of the dough as uniform as possible to ensure even baking. Sprinkle with coarse salt.

5. Place the pan on the middle rack of the cold oven. Turn the oven on to 400°F. Bake for 12 to 15 minutes, until the top is golden brown and firm. Cool the bread in the pan on a wire rack for 10 minutes. Transfer to a cutting board. Brush lightly with olive oil (if you like) and dust with Parmesan. Top with arugula (if using), then cut or tear the bread into 8 pieces. Serve warm with the dipping oil.

Per piece: 115 calories; 2g protein; 6g total fat; 1g fiber; 13g carbohydrates; 24mg cholesterol; 85mg sodium

Preparation time: 15 minutes
Rising time: about 35 to 45 minutes
Baking time: 30 to 35 minutes

French Baguette

(V)

Nothing beats a freshly baked French baguette. To make this bread more quickly (by skipping the rising time) and have a smoother crust, try the cold-oven method outlined below.

MAKES 10 SLICES
(ONE 12-INCH BAGUETTE)

1 tablespoon active dry yeast

1½ teaspoons granulated sugar, divided

1 cup warm (110°F) milk of choice

1 cup Carol's Gluten-Free Flour Blend (page 24)

½ cup potato starch (or cornstarch for a smoother crust)

1 teaspoon xanthan gum

¾ teaspoon salt

1½ teaspoons unsalted butter, buttery spread, or canola oil, at room temperature

2 large egg whites, beaten thoroughly until foamy, at room temperature, divided

½ teaspoon cider vinegar

1 teaspoon sesame seeds, for sprinkling (optional)

1. Dissolve the yeast and ½ teaspoon of the sugar in the warm milk. Set aside until foamy, about 5 minutes.

2. Line one trench of a nonstick French baguette pan (gray, not black) with parchment paper. (If the pan is perforated, it must be lined with parchment paper or the soft dough will fall through the perforations.)

3. In a medium bowl, combine the yeast-milk mixture, the remaining 1 teaspoon sugar, the flour blend, potato starch, xanthan gum, salt, butter, three-fourths of the egg whites, and the vinegar. With an electric mixer (using regular beaters, not dough hooks), beat on low speed just until blended. Increase the speed to medium-low and beat for 30 seconds, scraping down the sides of the bowl with a spatula. The dough will be soft.

4. With a wet spatula, smooth the dough into a 12-inch log in the parchment-lined trench, making the ends blunt rather than tapered for more even baking. Whisk the remaining egg whites with a tablespoon of water and brush on the dough; it helps make a glossier crust. Let the dough rise at room temperature (75°F to 85°F) until doubled in height, 35 to 45 minutes. Bread rises at different rates, depending on altitude, temperature, and humidity, so your bread may take more or less time to rise.

5. While the bread rises, preheat the oven to 425°F. Just before baking, make 3 diagonal slashes (⅛ inch deep) in the loaf so steam can escape during baking. Sprinkle with the sesame seeds, if using.

6. Bake on a rack in the middle of the oven until nicely browned and an instant-read thermometer registers 200°F to 205°F when inserted into the center of the loaf, 30 to 35 minutes. Tent with aluminum foil after 20 minutes of baking to prevent over-browning. Remove the bread from the pan; cool completely on a wire rack before slicing with a serrated knife or electric knife.

COLD OVEN METHOD FOR FRENCH BAGUETTE Starting bread to bake in a cold oven produces a smoother, crispier crust and a more irregular but attractive artisan-like crumb. The crust is crispier because it dries out a bit as the oven preheats.

Here is how to do it: Do not preheat the oven. Place the pan of unrisen bread on a rack in the middle of the oven; then turn on the oven to 425°F. Bake the baguette until its crust is nicely browned and an instant-read thermometer registers 200°F to 205°F when inserted into the center of the loaf, 35 to 40 minutes. Lay a sheet of aluminum foil over the bread after 15 minutes of baking if it starts to brown too much.

This method works perfectly in my KitchenAid wall oven, but it doesn't work in all ovens—especially those with quick preheating. Nor does it work with traditional-size loaves (such as 5x9-inch or 4x8-inch), because they are too thick. Try it once in your oven; if it doesn't work, then use the traditional method of rising the bread outlined in Step 4.

WHAT ABOUT LEFTOVERS? You can keep leftover baguette for a day, tightly sealed on your kitchen counter. If you still have leftovers after a day, freeze the loaf, make croutons or bread crumbs, or cut thin slices and toast the slices for crostini.

Per slice: 115 calories; 2g protein; 1g total fat; 1g fiber; 21g carbohydrates; 3mg cholesterol; 199mg sodium

Desserts

It's no secret that I live by this motto: "Life is short. Eat dessert first." Now, technically I don't actually do that (okay, maybe once in a while . . .), but when I'm in a restaurant, I always check the dessert menu before I choose my main dish. If the dessert options look good, then I make sure I'm not too full to enjoy it. I want to savor every bite.

So, given my infatuation with sweets, I took particular joy in carving down these recipes to two servings. I chose recipes that require considerable math to downsize with success; they include many old favorites such as cookies, bars, cakes, cupcakes, cheesecakes, pies, and puddings—and a few of my favorites that defy classification, such as Tiramisu, crepes, and pavlova. Also, I include frostings that contain few ingredients yet require perfect ratios to make them work.

The good news about perfectly portioned desserts for two is that you won't have a huge Bundt cake or 48 cookies sitting around for days. Instead, you can savor a small parcel of something delicious and be done with it. Until the next time. So indulge yourself and enjoy these delicious desserts.

Preparation time: 10 minutes
Chilling time: 1 hour
Baking time: 10 to 12 minutes

Chocolate Chip Cookies

Chocolate chip cookies are one of America's favorites. This eight-cookie recipe lets small households indulge without being overwhelmed. I like mini chocolate chips here, but regular chips work well, too.

MAKES 8 COOKIES

½ cup Carol's Gluten-Free Flour Blend (page 24)

½ teaspoon xanthan gum

¹⁄₁₆ teaspoon (pinch) baking soda

¹⁄₁₆ teaspoon (pinch) salt (or ¹⁄₃₂ teaspoon/smidgen if using buttery spread)

1 tablespoon unsalted butter or buttery spread (not diet or whipped)

¼ cup granulated sugar

3 tablespoons packed brown sugar

1 large egg yolk

½ teaspoon pure vanilla extract

1 to 2 teaspoons water, as needed

3 tablespoons gluten-free mini chocolate chips (see below)

2 tablespoons finely chopped walnuts

1. In a small bowl, whisk together the flour blend, xanthan gum, baking soda, and salt. In a medium bowl with an electric mixer on low speed, beat the butter, granulated sugar, and brown sugar until completely blended. Add the egg yolk and vanilla and beat until thoroughly blended. Gradually beat in the flour mixture until a stiff dough forms. If you can shape the dough into a ball with your hands, it's ready. If a dough doesn't form, add water—1 teaspoon at a time—until it does. Then, beat in the chocolate chips and walnuts to make a stiff dough. Shape into a 1-inch-thick disk, cover, and chill for 1 hour.

2. Place a rack in the center of the oven. Preheat the oven to 375°F. Line a 9x13-inch baking sheet (not nonstick) with parchment paper.

3. Divide the dough into 8 equal portions, shape each portion into a ball, and place the balls 2 inches apart on the baking sheet.

4. Bake the cookies until browned around the edges, 10 to 12 minutes. Cool for 2 to 3 minutes on the baking sheet on a wire rack; then use a thin metal spatula to transfer the cookies to the rack to cool completely.

GLUTEN IN CHOCOLATE CHIPS Chocolate chips are generally gluten free, but there are brands (usually found in natural food stores) sweetened with barley malt that you must avoid; always read the labels.

Per cookie: 135 calories; 1g protein; 5g total fat; 1g fiber; 23g carbohydrates; 30mg cholesterol; 41mg sodium

Coconut Macaroons

Next to chocolate, coconut is my favorite flavor, so why not combine the two? For chocolate-dipped macaroons, melt 4 ounces of bittersweet chocolate chips with ½ teaspoon butter until smooth. Dip the cooled cookies in the warm chocolate and let stand for 25 minutes to firm up. Heaven . . .

MAKES 4 COOKIES

1 large egg white

2 tablespoons granulated sugar

¼ teaspoon pure vanilla extract

¼ teaspoon pure coconut extract (optional)

¹⁄₃₂ teaspoon (smidgen) salt

1 cup tightly packed sweetened shredded coconut

1. Place a rack in the center of the oven. Preheat the oven to 350°F. Line a 7x10-inch rimmed baking sheet (not nonstick) with parchment paper.

2. In a medium bowl (or a 4-cup glass Pyrex measuring cup), with an electric mixer on medium speed, beat the egg white until foamy and airy, about 1 minute. Add the sugar, vanilla, coconut extract (if using), and salt and beat just until blended. Add the coconut and beat just until well blended. The dough will look somewhat coarse and raggedy, but that's okay.

3. With wet hands or a #30 spring-action ice cream scoop, shape the dough loosely into 4 balls, each about 1½ inches in diameter, and drop 2 inches apart on the baking sheet.

4. Bake until the cookies are browned around the edges, 20 to 25 minutes. Cool the cookies on the baking sheet on a wire rack for 10 minutes, then use a thin metal spatula to transfer the cookies to the rack to cool completely.

Per cookie: 115 calories; 1g protein; 6g total fat; 1g fiber; 15g carbohydrates; 0mg cholesterol; 70mg sodium

Preparation time: 10 minutes
Chilling time: 2 hours
Baking time: 10 to 12 minutes

Chocolate–Peanut Butter Cookies

(V)

What tastes better than chocolate or peanut butter? Those two heavenly flavors combined in this decadent little cookie. If you don't want to bake all 12 cookies right away, shape the dough into balls and freeze a few for later baking. For best results, use regular or mini chocolate chips rather than the large size. This recipe calls for only one flour (rather than a blend of flours); use it to experiment with new flours.

MAKES 12 COOKIES

1 cup (6 ounces) bittersweet chocolate chips (at least 60% cacao), divided (see Gluten in Chocolate Chips, page 176)

1 tablespoon creamy peanut butter

1 teaspoon unsalted butter, buttery spread, or coconut oil

1 large egg

⅓ cup granulated sugar

¼ cup brown rice flour (or your favorite flour)

¹⁄₁₆ teaspoon (pinch) baking soda

¹⁄₁₆ teaspoon (pinch) xanthan gum

¹⁄₃₂ teaspoon (smidgen) salt

¼ cup finely chopped walnuts or peanuts

1. In a small microwave-safe bowl, heat ¼ cup of the chocolate chips, the peanut butter, and butter on Low power in the microwave oven for about 30 seconds, until melted. Stir; set aside to cool.

2. In a separate small bowl, with an electric mixer on low speed, beat the egg, sugar, flour, baking soda, xanthan gum, and salt until well blended. Beat in the melted chocolate mixture until no flour streaks remain. Stir in the walnuts and remaining chocolate chips. The dough will be soft. Refrigerate, covered, for 2 hours.

3. Place a rack in the middle of the oven and preheat the oven to 375°F. Line a 9x13-inch baking sheet (not nonstick) with parchment paper.

continued~

4. Shape the dough into 12 walnut-sized balls and place on the baking sheet at least 1½ inches apart. Bake just until the tops start to crack, 10 to 12 minutes. Do not overbake. Cool the cookies 2 minutes on the baking sheet on a wire rack, then use a thin metal spatula to transfer the cookies to the rack to cool completely.

MAKE-AHEAD CHOCOLATE–PEANUT BUTTER COOKIES To freeze the dough for baking later, place the dough balls on a parchment-lined baking sheet and place in the freezer. When frozen, transfer the balls to a freezer-safe container and freeze for up to 1 month. When you're ready to bake, thaw the dough balls and bake as directed on a parchment-lined baking sheet.

Per cookie: 135 calories; 2g protein; 7g total fat; 1g fiber; 18g carbohydrates; 16mg cholesterol; 20mg sodium

Preparation time: 10 minutes
Chilling time: 1 hour
Baking time: 20 to 25 minutes

Spice Cookies

(V)

Spicy and aromatic, these heavenly little orbs are good on their own, crumbled into a no-bake pie crust, or as a topping for fruit desserts. They also travel well. Years ago, I carried a batch in my suitcase to a book signing event that was a thousand miles away and they arrived in perfect shape. They are perfect for holidays, when the aroma signifies celebration.

MAKES 8 COOKIES

¼ cup packed brown sugar

2 tablespoons unsalted butter or buttery spread, at room temperature

1 tablespoon molasses (not blackstrap)

½ teaspoon pure vanilla extract

½ cup Carol's Gluten-Free Flour Blend (page 24)

2 tablespoons cornstarch

¾ teaspoon ground cinnamon

¾ teaspoon ground ginger

½ teaspoon baking soda

½ teaspoon xanthan gum

¼ teaspoon salt (or ⅛ teaspoon/ dash if using buttery spread)

⅛ teaspoon (dash) ground nutmeg

⅛ teaspoon (dash) ground cloves

1 to 2 teaspoons water, if needed

1. In a food processor, process the brown sugar, butter, molasses, and vanilla until thoroughly blended. Add all of the remaining ingredients except the water. Process until the dough forms a ball on one side of the bowl. Add water, 1 teaspoon at a time, only if the dough fails to form a ball. (Alternately, use an electric mixer to mix the dough, and add water, 1 teaspoon at a time, until the dough holds together when you press a tablespoon of it into a ball.) Shape the dough into a 1-inch-thick disk, wrap tightly, and refrigerate for 1 hour.

2. Place a rack in the center of the oven. Preheat the oven to 325°F. Line a 9x13-inch rimmed baking sheet (not nonstick) with parchment paper.

3. With your hands, shape the dough into eight 1-inch balls and place on the baking sheet at least 1½ inches apart. Flatten each ball slightly with the flat side of a wet spatula.

4. Bake until the cookies start to brown on the bottom, 20 to 25 minutes. Cool the cookies on the baking sheet on a wire rack for 5 minutes, then use a thin metal spatula to transfer the cookies to the rack to cool completely.

Per cookie: 100 calories; 1g protein; 3g total fat; 1g fiber; 18g carbohydrates; 8mg cholesterol; 161mg sodium

Preparation time: 10 minutes
Baking time: 15 to 18 minutes
per batch (two batches)

Oatmeal-Raisin Cookies ⓥ

If you like, replace the raisins with the same amount of chocolate chips, which is equally delicious. If you're indecisive, or just want to mix it up a bit, use half raisins and half chocolate chips.

MAKES 12 COOKIES

⅔ cup packed brown sugar

2 tablespoons cold unsalted butter or buttery spread

½ teaspoon pure vanilla extract

1 large egg

1 cup Carol's Gluten-Free Flour Blend (page 24)

½ teaspoon xanthan gum

⅛ teaspoon (dash) baking soda

½ teaspoon ground cinnamon

¼ teaspoon salt (or ⅛ teaspoon/dash if using butter spread)

¾ cup gluten-free rolled oats*

½ cup raisins

1. Place a rack in the center of the oven. Preheat the oven to 375°F. Line a 9x13-inch baking sheet (not nonstick) with parchment paper.

2. In a medium bowl, with an electric mixer on low speed, beat the brown sugar, butter, and vanilla together until smooth. Beat in the egg until well blended. In a small bowl, whisk together the flour blend, xanthan gum, baking soda, cinnamon, and salt until thoroughly blended. Beat the dry ingredients into the butter-sugar mixture on low speed until no flour streaks remain. Beat in the oats and raisins. The dough will be stiff.

3. Drop twelve 2-tablespoon-sized balls at least 1½ inches apart on the baking sheet. (For uniform-size balls, use a #30 ice cream scoop or a 2-tablespoon measuring spoon.) For thinner cookies, flatten the dough with a wet spatula to a ½-inch thickness before baking.

4. Bake until the edges of the cookies are firm and lightly browned, 15 to 18 minutes. Cool the cookies on the baking sheet on a wire rack for 5 minutes, then use a thin metal spatula to transfer the cookies to the rack to cool completely. Repeat with remaining dough.

Check with your physician to make sure gluten-free oats are right for your diet.

Per cookie: 155 calories; 2g protein; 3g total fat; 1g fiber; 30g carbohydrates; 21mg cholesterol; 78mg sodium

Preparation time: 10 minutes
Chilling time: 1 hour
Baking time: 18 to 20 minutes

Peanut Butter Cookies (V)

Peanut butter lovers adore these all-American cookies. The recipe makes 12 cookies, enough to feed your peanut-butter lust, with a few left over for snacking later or to crumble into parfaits or on top of puddings. Or, put a banana slice between two cookies for a cookie sandwich.

MAKES 12 COOKIES

⅓ cup crunchy peanut butter

½ cup granulated sugar

1 large egg

½ teaspoon pure vanilla extract

⅔ cup Carol's Gluten-Free Flour Blend (page 24)

1 tablespoon cornstarch

¼ teaspoon xanthan gum

¼ teaspoon baking soda

⅛ teaspoon (dash) salt (or ¼ teaspoon if using unsalted peanut butter)

1. In a medium bowl, with an electric mixer on low speed, beat the peanut butter, sugar, egg, and vanilla until well blended.

2. In a small bowl, whisk together the flour blend, cornstarch, xanthan gum, baking soda, and salt until well blended. Gradually beat the dry ingredients into the peanut butter mixture until a stiff dough forms. Shape the dough into a disk and refrigerate, tightly wrapped, for 1 hour.

3. Place a rack in the center of the oven. Preheat the oven to 375°F. Line a 9x13-inch baking sheet (not nonstick) with parchment paper.

4. Shape the dough into twelve 1-inch balls (or for uniform cookies, use a #50 metal ice cream scoop). Place the balls 2 inches apart on the baking sheet. Flatten cookies slightly with the tines of a fork in a crisscross pattern.

5. Bake until the cookie edges start to brown, 18 to 20 minutes. Cool the cookies on the baking sheet on a wire rack for 5 minutes, then use a thin metal spatula to transfer the cookies to the rack to cool completely.

Per cookie: 115 calories; 2g protein; 4g total fat; 1g fiber; 17g carbohydrates; 16mg cholesterol; 94mg sodium

Preparation time: 10 minutes
Chilling time: 1 hour or overnight
Baking time: 12 to 15 minutes

Sugar Cut-Out Cookies

This recipe makes a not-too-sweet cookie for cut-outs that just beg for your favorite icing—or holiday decorating. For best results, use a metal (rather than plastic) cookie cutter for a sharp edge, and be sure to roll the dough to an even thickness so the cookies brown at the same rate.

MAKES 12 (2-INCH) COOKIES

1 cup Carol's Gluten-Free Flour Blend (page 24)

½ cup plus 1 tablespoon granulated sugar

¼ cup (4 tablespoons) cold unsalted butter or buttery spread, cut into 4 pieces

3 tablespoons cornstarch

½ teaspoon xanthan gum

¼ teaspoon salt (or ⅛ teaspoon/dash if using buttery spread)

1/16 teaspoon (pinch) baking powder

1 large egg

1 teaspoon pure vanilla extract or almond extract

1 to 2 teaspoons water, if needed

1. In a medium mixing bowl, with an electric mixer on low speed, beat the flour blend, all the sugar, butter, cornstarch, xanthan gum, salt, and baking powder until the mixture resembles dry peas. Beat in the egg and vanilla for 2 minutes, until a stiff dough forms. If the mixture is dry and clumpy, beat in water, 1 teaspoon at a time, until the dough holds together without crumbling when you squeeze it in your fingers. (Alternatively, blend the dry ingredients and butter in a small food processor, and then blend in the egg and vanilla and process until a stiff dough forms, adding water, 1 teaspoon at a time, only if needed to make a dough that holds together without crumbling.) Shape the dough into a 1-inch disk, wrap it tightly in foil or plastic wrap, and refrigerate for at least 1 hour or overnight.

2. Place a rack in the middle of the oven. Preheat the oven to 375°F. Line a 9x13-inch baking sheet (not nonstick) with parchment paper.

3. Keep the dough chilled until you are ready to roll it out. Place the chilled dough on a 12-inch square of parchment paper. Cut a piece of plastic wrap the same size, lay it on top of the dough, and roll the dough ¼ inch thick. Remove the plastic wrap and cut out cookies with a 2-inch cookie cutter, reserving the scraps. With a thin metal spatula, arrange the cookies at least 1 inch apart on the baking sheet. If the cookies are too soft to handle,

place the parchment paper (with cookies on it) in the freezer for 10 minutes, then try again. Reroll the scraps, cut more cookies, and arrange on the baking sheet. If your sheet won't hold all of the cookies, bake them in two batches, keeping the unbaked cookies chilled until ready to bake.

4. Bake for 12 to 15 minutes, until the edges are lightly browned, rotating the sheet halfway through baking. Cool the cookies on the baking sheet on a wire rack for 2 minutes, then use a thin metal spatula to transfer the cookies to the rack to cool completely.

DECORATING THE COOKIES To make the cookies extra special, frost and then decorate as desired with sprinkles, coconut, raisins, chocolate chips, or whatever you like. See the frosting recipes starting on page 226.

Per cookie: 130 calories; 1g protein; 4g total fat; 1g fiber; 21g carbohydrates; 26mg cholesterol; 64mg sodium

Chocolate Brownies

Fudgy and chewy, these decadent brownies are decidedly addictive. They are good plain, dusted with powdered sugar, or topped with a rich chocolate frosting (page 228). Or, top with ice cream, fudge sauce, and a bright red maraschino cherry for a brownie sundae. Enjoy!!

MAKES 8 (2-INCH)
BROWNIES

½ cup Carol's Gluten-
Free Flour Blend
(page 24)

¼ cup unsweetened
natural cocoa powder
(not Dutch-processed)

½ teaspoon xanthan
gum

¼ teaspoon salt (or
⅛ teaspoon/dash if
using buttery spread)

¼ cup unsalted butter or
buttery spread, melted
and cooled slightly

¼ cup granulated sugar

¼ cup packed brown
sugar

1 large egg, at room
temperature

½ teaspoon pure vanilla
extract

1. Place a rack in the center of the oven. Preheat the oven to 350°F. Generously grease a 4x8-inch nonstick loaf pan (gray, not black). Line the pan with parchment paper or aluminum foil, leaving a 2-inch "handle" on two opposite sides for lifting the brownies out of the pan.

2. In a small bowl, whisk together the flour blend, cocoa, xanthan gum, and salt until well blended. In a medium bowl, with an electric mixer on low speed, beat the butter and both sugars until well combined. Add the egg and vanilla and beat until well combined. Gradually beat in the flour mixture to make a stiff batter. Spread the batter evenly in the pan.

3. Bake for 15 minutes, or until the edges are firm but some crumbs cling to a toothpick inserted into the center. The brownies continue to cook after they come out of the oven. Do not overbake or the brownies won't be fudgy. Cool the brownies completely in the pan on a wire rack. Lift the brownies out of the pan with the parchment handles. Cut into 8 (2-inch) brownies.

Per brownie: 150 calories; 2g protein; 7g total fat; 1g fiber;
22g carbohydrates; 39mg cholesterol; 89mg sodium

Lemon Bars

Ⓥ

This the classic lemon bar, downsized to two cute little squares of sheer delight. I'm not sure why, but I like to serve these tart/sweet bars after a Mexican meal. It just seems right!

MAKES 2 BARS

Crust
3 tablespoons Carol's Gluten-Free Flour Blend (page 24)

1 tablespoon powdered sugar, plus more for dusting

1/32 teaspoon (smidgen) xanthan gum

1/32 teaspoon (smidgen) salt

1 tablespoon cold unsalted butter or buttery spread

Filling
2 large egg yolks

1 teaspoon grated lemon zest

2 tablespoons fresh lemon juice

1/4 cup granulated sugar

2 teaspoons Carol's Gluten-Free Flour Blend (page 24)

1/32 teaspoon (smidgen) xanthan gum

1/32 teaspoon (smidgen) salt

1. Preheat the oven to 350°F. Generously grease a 3¼x5¾-inch nonstick loaf pan (gray, not black). Cut a piece of parchment paper or foil 5 inches wide and 12 inches long and position in the pan, leaving a 2-inch "handle" on the long sides for lifting the bars out of the pan.

2. Make the crust: In a small bowl, whisk together the flour blend, powdered sugar, xanthan gum, and salt. With a fork, cut in the butter until the mixture resembles peas. With your fingers, press the dough evenly into the bottom of the pan. Bake until the edges are lightly browned, 8 to 10 minutes. Watch carefully—the crust can burn quickly because it is so small and thin. Cool 10 minutes in the pan on a wire rack.

3. Meanwhile, make the filling: In the same bowl, whisk together the egg yolks, lemon zest, and lemon juice until completely smooth. In a very small bowl, whisk together the sugar, flour blend, xanthan gum, and salt until well blended; whisk the dry mixture into the egg mixture until smooth.

4. Pour the filling over the crust. Bake until the filling looks firm, 15 to 18 minutes. Cool the bars completely in the pan on a wire rack. Using the parchment paper handles, gently transfer the bars from the pan to a cutting board. To serve, dust with powdered sugar and use a sharp knife to cut into two bars.

Per bar: 315 calories; 4g protein; 11g total fat; 1g fiber; 49g carbohydrates; 228mg cholesterol; 81mg sodium

Chocolate Cake in a Cup (V)

These cute little individual cakes are just perfect for couples, and they are super quick. They can be eaten right out of the coffee cup, almost immediately after they come out of the microwave, although a little bit of cooling time is a good idea.

MAKES 2 INDIVIDUAL CAKES

⅓ cup Carol's Gluten-Free Flour Blend (page 24)

3 tablespoons granulated sugar

2 tablespoons unsweetened natural cocoa (not Dutch-processed)

⅛ teaspoon (dash) baking powder

⅛ teaspoon (dash) salt

1 large egg, at room temperature

2 tablespoons canola oil

1 tablespoon water

½ teaspoon pure vanilla extract

Powdered sugar or chocolate syrup, for garnish

1. Generously grease 2 shallow, microwave-safe 6-ounce (¾-cup) coffee cups. (My coffee cups are 3¼ inches in diameter and 2¼ inches high. The batter may spill over the edge during baking if you use a smaller cup.)

2. In a small bowl, whisk together the flour blend, sugar, cocoa, baking powder, and salt until well blended, and then whisk in the egg, oil, water, and vanilla until smooth. The batter will be soft. Divide the batter between the two coffee cups and place the cups on saucers or plates to catch any drips.

3. Microwave on medium-high (70%) power for 50 to 60 seconds. The cakes are done when they look firm and are no longer shiny on top. They will continue to cook after they are out of the microwave. The cooking time may vary depending on the wattage of your microwave oven. Cool slightly before eating right out of the cup, dusted with powdered sugar or drizzled with chocolate syrup—or both!

Per cake: 335 calories; 5g protein; 17g total fat; 3g fiber; 42g carbohydrates; 94mg cholesterol; 215mg sodium

Mom's Chocolate Cake ⓥ

This was my mother's cake recipe and our family of five ate it all through my childhood. Oh, the memories! Whenever we asked my mother for chocolate cake, this was the recipe. I then raised my son on Mom's cake and it remains one of our family favorites. I have downsized it to make a 5-inch cake that is better suited to a small household. You can eat it plain, dusted with powdered sugar, or frosted (see the frosting recipes starting on page 226).

MAKES 4 SMALL SLICES
(ONE 5-INCH CAKE)

¼ cup Carol's Gluten-Free Flour Blend (page 24)

¼ cup granulated sugar

2 tablespoons plus 1 teaspoon unsweetened natural cocoa (not Dutch-processed)

¼ teaspoon salt

⅛ teaspoon (dash) baking soda

⅛ teaspoon (dash) xanthan gum

1 large egg, at room temperature

2 tablespoons canola oil

2 tablespoons water

½ teaspoon pure vanilla extract

1. Place a rack in the middle position of the oven. Preheat the oven to 350°F. Generously grease a 5-inch nonstick springform cake pan (gray, not black) or a 5-inch cake pan (gray, not black). Line the bottom of the pan with parchment paper, and then grease the parchment.

2. In a small bowl, whisk together the flour blend, sugar, cocoa, salt, baking soda, and xanthan gum until well blended. With an electric mixer on low speed, beat in the egg, oil, water, and vanilla until blended. Spread the batter evenly in the pan.

3. Bake until a toothpick inserted into the center of the cake comes out clean, 20 to 22 minutes. Cool the cake completely in the pan on a wire rack. Remove the cake from the pan and transfer to a plate. Cut into 4 pieces to serve.

Per slice: 165 calories; 2g protein; 8g total fat; 1g fiber; 22g carbohydrates; 47mg cholesterol; 190mg sodium

Flourless Chocolate Cake

This dessert is perfect for those who don't eat grains. A simple dusting of powdered sugar is elegant, and a pretty garnish of fresh berries and mint leaves completes this showstopper dessert. You could also serve it with whipped topping or your favorite frosting (see frosting recipes starting on page 226).

MAKES 4 SMALL SLICES
(ONE 5-INCH CAKE)

²/₃ cup almond meal/
flour or hazelnut meal/
flour

¼ cup packed light
brown sugar

2 tablespoons plus
1 teaspoon unsweetened
natural cocoa (not
Dutch-processed)

¹/₁₆ teaspoon (pinch)
baking soda

¹/₁₆ teaspoon (pinch)
xanthan gum

¹/₁₆ teaspoon (pinch) salt

1 large egg, at room
temperature

2 tablespoons canola oil

½ teaspoon pure vanilla
extract

Powdered sugar, for
garnish

Garnishes of your
choice: raspberries,
strawberries, mint leaves

1. Place a rack in the middle of the oven. Preheat the oven to 325°F. Generously grease a 5-inch nonstick springform pan (gray, not black). Line the bottom with parchment paper, and then grease the parchment.

2. In a medium bowl, whisk together the almond meal/flour, brown sugar, cocoa, baking soda, xanthan gum, and salt until well blended. With an electric mixer on low speed, beat in the egg, oil, and vanilla until the mixture forms a smooth but stiff batter. Spread the batter evenly in the pan.

3. Bake until the top is firm and smooth and the cake starts to pull away from the edge of the pan, 20 to 25 minutes. Cool the cake for 10 minutes in the pan on a wire rack. Gently run a knife around the edge of the pan to loosen the cake. Remove the outer rim. Cool the cake, still on the bottom of the springform pan, on the wire rack.

4. To serve, run a knife between the pan bottom and cake to loosen. Invert the cake onto a serving platter and remove the parchment. Dust with powdered sugar, cut into four slices, and serve garnished with berries and mint leaves.

Flourless Cupcakes: If you don't have a 5-inch springform pan, make cupcakes: Line 4 cups of a 6-cup standard nonstick muffin pan (gray, not black) with paper liners. Divide the batter among the four cups and bake until a toothpick inserted into the center comes out clean, 20 to 25 minutes.

Per slice: 230 calories; 11g protein; 12g total fat; 1g fiber;
22g carbohydrates; 47mg cholesterol; 87mg sodium

Gingerbread

Decidedly aromatic, this spicy gingerbread fills your kitchen with delicious smells . . . making it the perfect dessert for a crisp autumn day. It keeps nicely on the countertop, so you can enjoy it for a couple of days after baking. Topped with a dollop of whipped cream and a twist of lemon, it's divine.

MAKES 4 SLICES
(ONE 3¼x5¾-INCH LOAF)

⅓ cup Carol's Gluten-Free Flour Blend (page 24)

3 tablespoons packed brown sugar

¼ teaspoon xanthan gum

¼ teaspoon ground ginger

¼ teaspoon ground cinnamon

¼ teaspoon ground cloves

⅛ teaspoon (dash) baking powder

⅛ teaspoon (dash) salt

¹⁄₁₆ teaspoon (pinch) baking soda

¹⁄₁₆ teaspoon (pinch) ground nutmeg

2 tablespoons canola oil

2 tablespoons molasses

1 large egg, at room temperature

1. Place a rack in the middle of the oven. Preheat the oven to 350°F. Generously grease a 3¼x5¾-inch nonstick loaf pan (gray, not black).

2. In a medium bowl, whisk together the flour blend, brown sugar, xanthan gum, ginger, cinnamon, cloves, baking powder, salt, baking soda, and nutmeg until well blended. With an electric mixer on low speed, beat in the oil, molasses, and egg until well blended, about 30 seconds. Spread the batter evenly in the pan.

3. Bake until a toothpick inserted into the center of the gingerbread comes out clean, 20 to 25 minutes. Cool the gingerbread in the pan on a wire rack for 20 minutes. Cut into four slices, and serve slightly warm.

Per slice: 190 calories; 2g protein; 8g total fat; 1g fiber; 28g carbohydrates; 47mg cholesterol; 129mg sodium

Preparation time: 10 minutes
Baking time: 25 to 30 minutes

Vanilla Mini-Bundt Cake

This cake is the LBD ("little black dress") of desserts because it's so very versatile (see variation, below). Dust the cake with powdered sugar or drizzle frosting on top (see frosting recipes, starting on page 226). Bundt cake pans in 3-cup sizes are available online or at specialty kitchen stores.

MAKES 6 SMALL SLICES
(ONE 6-INCH BUNDT CAKE)

2 tablespoons unsalted butter or buttery spread, at room temperature

1 tablespoon canola oil

1 tablespoon sour cream or sour cream alternative

⅓ cup granulated sugar

1 large egg, at room temperature

¼ teaspoon pure vanilla extract

¾ cup Carol's Gluten-Free Flour Blend (page 24)

½ teaspoon baking powder

¼ teaspoon xanthan gum

¼ teaspoon salt (or ⅛ teaspoon/ dash if using buttery spread)

1⁄16 teaspoon (pinch) baking soda

Powdered sugar, for garnish

Fresh fruit, such as raspberries, blueberries, or strawberries, for garnish

1. Place a rack in the middle of the oven. Preheat the oven to 325°F. Generously grease a 3-cup nonstick Bundt pan (gray, not black) with solid vegetable shortening.

2. In a medium bowl, with the mixer on low speed, beat the butter, oil, sour cream, and sugar until well blended, about 1 minute. Beat in the egg and vanilla for 30 seconds.

3. In a small bowl, whisk together the flour blend, baking powder, xanthan gum, salt, and baking soda until well blended. Gradually beat the flour mixture into the egg mixture on low speed, until well blended, about 30 seconds. Spread the batter evenly in the pan.

4. Bake until the top is golden brown and a toothpick inserted into the center comes out clean, 25 to 30 minutes. Cool the cake in the pan on a wire rack for 10 minutes. Run a sharp knife around the edges to loosen the cake. Remove the cake from the pan and cool on the wire rack. Garnish with powdered sugar and fresh fruit.

Lemon–Poppy Seed Mini-Bundt Cake: Add 1½ teaspoons poppy seeds and ¾ teaspoon lemon zest. Bake as directed.

Per slice: 180 calories; 2g protein; 7g total fat; 1g fiber; 26g carbohydrates; 42mg cholesterol; 157mg sodium

Red Velvet Cupcakes

The popularity of these gorgeous little gems may have peaked years ago, but I still think they are luscious enough to include in this book. After all, most of us grew up eating red velvet cake. If your paper liners are small, you may get five cupcakes instead of four.

MAKES 4 OR 5 CUPCAKES

⅓ cup Carol's Gluten-Free Flour Blend (page 24)

⅓ cup granulated sugar

1 tablespoon unsweetened natural cocoa (not Dutch-processed)

¼ teaspoon xanthan gum

⅛ teaspoon (dash) baking soda

⅛ teaspoon (dash) salt

1 large egg, at room temperature

2 tablespoons canola oil

2 tablespoons water, at room temperature

½ teaspoon liquid red food coloring

½ teaspoon pure vanilla extract

Cream Cheese Frosting or your choice of frostings starting on page 226

1. Place a rack in the middle of the oven. Preheat the oven to 350°F. Line 4 (or 5) cups of a 6-cup standard nonstick muffin pan (gray, not black) with paper liners.

2. In a small mixing bowl, whisk together the flour blend, sugar, cocoa, xanthan gum, baking soda, and salt until well blended. With an electric mixer on low speed, beat in the egg, oil, water, food coloring, and vanilla until well blended. Spoon about 3 tablespoons of batter into each liner.

3. Bake until a toothpick inserted into the center of a cupcake comes out clean, 18 to 20 minutes. Cool the cupcakes in the pan on a wire rack for 10 minutes. Remove the cupcakes from the pan and cool completely on the rack. Frost with the cream cheese frosting or other favorite frosting. Refrigerate leftovers.

Per cupcake (¼ of recipe) with Cream Cheese Frosting (page 226): 330 calories; 3g protein; 10g total fat; 1g fiber; 59g carbohydrates; 51mg cholesterol; 177mg sodium

Carrot Cake Cupcakes

Most carrot cakes are huge—way too much for small households. But there's no reason you can't enjoy carrot cake—one of America's favorite flavors—in cupcake form. Yes, there are lots of ingredients, but that's what makes carrot cake so yummy. By the way, this recipe makes six cupcakes—more than most recipes in the book—because otherwise you'd be measuring extremely small amounts of ingredients and that gets tedious. Freeze the extras or invite friends over for dessert.

MAKES 6 CUPCAKES OR
ONE 6½- TO 7-INCH CAKE

Batter

¾ cup Carol's Gluten-Free Flour Blend (page 24)

¼ cup granulated sugar

¼ cup packed light brown sugar

1 teaspoon ground cinnamon

½ teaspoon xanthan gum

¼ teaspoon baking soda

¼ teaspoon salt

1 large egg, at room temperature

3 tablespoons canola oil

¼ cup crushed pineapple, drained thoroughly, 2 tablespoons juice reserved

½ cup finely shredded carrots

¼ cup sweetened shredded coconut

2 tablespoons finely chopped walnuts, divided

Cream Cheese Frosting or your choice of frostings starting on page 226

1. Place a rack in the middle of the oven. Preheat the oven to 325°F. Generously grease a 6-cup standard nonstick muffin pan (gray, not black) or line with paper liners. Or, generously grease a 6½- to 7-inch nonstick springform pan (gray, not black) and line with parchment paper, then grease the parchment.

2. Make the batter: In a medium bowl, whisk the flour blend, granulated sugar, brown sugar, cinnamon, xanthan gum, baking soda, and salt until well blended.

3. In a medium mixing bowl, with an electric mixer on low speed, beat the egg, oil, and the 2 tablespoons pineapple juice until smooth. Gradually beat in the flour mixture just until no flour streaks are visible. Stir in the pineapple, carrots, coconut, and 1 tablespoon of the chopped walnuts until completely blended. Divide the batter evenly among the muffin cups or spread evenly in the springform pan.

continued~

4. Bake the cupcakes for 25 to 30 minutes or the cake for 30 to 40 minutes, until a toothpick inserted into the center comes out clean. Cool in the pan on a wire rack for 10 minutes.

5. Remove the cupcakes from the pan and cool completely on the wire rack. For the cake, run a sharp knife around the edges to loosen the cake. Remove the outer rim. Cool the cake completely on the wire rack. Gently run a knife between the pan bottom and cake to loosen. Invert onto a serving plate and remove the parchment paper. Frost with the cream cheese frosting or other favorite frosting. Sprinkle with the remaining walnuts. Refrigerate leftovers.

LEFTOVER PINEAPPLE Add the leftover pineapple in a smoothie or use it in the Sweet-and-Sour Pork recipe on page 93.

Per serving with Cream Cheese Frosting (page 226): 340 calories; 3g protein; 12g total fat; 2g fiber; 56g carbohydrates; 37mg cholesterol; 181mg sodium

Cherry Cobbler

(V)

Canned tart red cherries (sometimes known as Montmorency cherries) are available year-round, so there's no reason for not making this homestyle dessert anytime of the year. However, if you can find fresh cherries straight from the tree (the way I first enjoyed cobbler when I was a child), you are indeed a lucky person.

MAKES 2 SERVINGS

Filling
¾ cup fresh or canned tart or sour red cherries, well drained if canned (half of a 14-ounce can)

2 tablespoons granulated sugar (or more or less, depending on tartness of cherries)

1 teaspoon quick-cooking tapioca

¼ teaspoon almond extract

¹⁄₃₂ teaspoon (smidgen) salt

Topping
½ cup Carol's Gluten-Free Flour Blend (page 24)

2 tablespoons granulated sugar, plus ½ teaspoon for sprinkling

¼ teaspoon baking powder

¹⁄₁₆ teaspoon (pinch) salt

1 tablespoon unsalted butter or buttery spread, melted and slightly cooled

1 large egg, at room temperature

1. Place a rack in the middle of the oven. Preheat the oven to 375°F. Generously grease two 3½x1¾-inch (4-ounce) ramekins.

2. Make the filling: In a small bowl, stir together the cherries, 2 tablespoons of sugar, the tapioca, almond extract, and salt. Divide evenly between the ramekins and let stand while preparing the topping.

3. Make the topping: In a small bowl, whisk together the flour blend, sugar, baking powder, and salt until well blended. With an electric mixer on low speed, beat in the butter, egg, and almond extract until just blended. Spread the batter evenly in the ramekins, and then sprinkle each with ¼ teaspoon sugar. Place the ramekins on a small rimmed baking sheet.

4. Bake until the topping is browned, 20 to 25 minutes. Cool the ramekins on a wire rack for 15 minutes. Serve warm.

Per serving: 300 calories; 4g protein; 8g total fat; 1g fiber; 55g carbohydrates; 109 mg cholesterol; 197mg sodium

Bing Cherry Clafoutis

You can use fresh, pitted Bing cherries (sometimes called dark or sweet cherries), or buy them canned or frozen. I make these single-serving clafoutis year-round, so in winter I use frozen Bing cherries. The recipe is quite versatile; feel free to vary the fruit.

MAKES 2 SERVINGS

½ cup fresh or frozen Bing cherries, thawed and drained if frozen

1 large egg, at room temperature

2 tablespoons milk of choice (the richer the better), at room temperature

1 tablespoon canola oil

1 teaspoon pure vanilla extract or pure almond extract

2½ tablespoons granulated sugar, plus 2 teaspoons for sprinkling

2 tablespoons Carol's Gluten-Free Flour Blend (page 24), or amaranth, millet, sorghum, or teff flour

1/16 teaspoon (pinch) salt

2 teaspoons sliced almonds

1 tablespoon powdered sugar, for dusting

1. Place a rack in the middle of the oven. Preheat the oven to 375°F. Generously grease two 3½x1¾-inch (4-ounce) ramekins.

2. Arrange the cherries in a single layer in each ramekin.

3. In a small bowl, whisk together the egg, milk, oil, and vanilla until very smooth. Gradually whisk in 2½ tablespoons of sugar, the flour blend, and salt until very smooth. Divide the batter between the ramekins, sprinkle with the almonds, and sprinkle with the remaining 2 teaspoons of sugar.

4. Bake until the tops are puffy and the almonds are golden brown, 20 to 25 minutes. Dust with powdered sugar. Serve immediately.

Chocolate-Cherry Clafoutis: Replace the vanilla with 1 teaspoon cherry brandy (kirschwasser) and add 1 tablespoon cocoa to the flour blend. Bake as directed.

Liqueur-Laced Clafoutis: For a festive touch, vary the fruit and add a teaspoon of a complementary liqueur to the batter. Some ideas to try:

- Cherries and cherry brandy (kirschwasser)
- Pears and pear liqueur
- Apricots and apricot brandy or hazelnut liqueur (Frangelico)
- Blueberries and lemon liqueur (limoncello) or orange liqueur (Grand Marnier or triple sec)

Per serving: 270 calories; 5g protein; 11g total fat; 2g fiber; 39g carbohydrates; 94mg cholesterol; 146mg sodium

Preparation time: 15 minutes + 15 minutes freezing time
Chilling time: 1 hour
Baking time: 45 to 50 minutes

Small Double-Crust Pie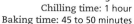

This recipe makes a cute little 5- or 6-inch double-crust pie perfect for two people. Using cow's milk (instead of nondairy versions) will make the crust brown the best. I include some of my favorite pie fillings on pages 204–205. Pies made with this crust recipe are best when eaten on the same day they are baked. I use a 5½-inch ceramic pie pan by Good Cook, available at grocery stores.

**MAKES 1 DOUBLE-CRUST
5- TO 6-INCH PIE**

½ cup Carol's Gluten-Free Flour Blend (page 24)

⅓ cup tapioca flour

¼ cup sweet rice flour

1 tablespoon granulated sugar plus ½ teaspoon for sprinkling

¼ teaspoon salt or ⅛ teaspoon (dash) if using buttery spread

⅛ teaspoon (dash) xanthan gum

1⁄16 teaspoon (pinch) baking soda

3 tablespoons butter-flavored shortening (I use Crisco)

2 tablespoons unsalted butter or buttery spread

3 tablespoons milk of choice, plus extra for brushing

1 to 2 teaspoons water, if needed

Filling of your choice (see Fillings for a 5- to 6-Inch Double Crust Pie on pages 204–205)

1. In a medium bowl, whisk together the flour blend, tapioca flour, sweet rice flour, 1 tablespoon sugar, the salt, xanthan gum, and baking soda until well blended. With an electric mixer on low speed, blend in the shortening, butter, and 3 tablespoons milk until the mixture forms small clumps. If you can shape the dough into a cohesive ball with your hands, it is ready. If not, beat in water, 1 teaspoon at a time, until the dough can be shaped into a ball without falling apart. Knead the dough with your hands until it is very smooth. Shape the dough into a 1-inch-thick disk, divide in half, wrap each half tightly with plastic wrap, and refrigerate for 1 hour, or freeze for up to 1 month.

2. Place racks in the bottom and middle positions of the oven. Preheat the oven to 375°F. Massage one disk of dough between your hands until it is pliable, which makes it easier to handle. With a rolling pin, roll the disk of dough into an 8-inch circle between two pieces of heavy-duty plastic wrap. (Use a damp paper towel between the countertop and bottom sheet of plastic wrap to prevent slipping.) To roll, move the rolling pin from the center of the dough to the outer edge, moving around the circle in clockwise fashion to assure uniform thickness of the crust so it bakes evenly.

3. Drape the crust over your hand, peel off the top plastic wrap, and invert the crust, centering it over a 5 to 6-inch pie pan. Remove the remaining plastic wrap and press the crust into place. Trim the edges to a 1-inch overhang all around the pan. Spread the filling evenly in the crust.

4. Roll the remaining dough to an 8-inch circle, again between two pieces of heavy-duty plastic wrap. Peel off the top sheet of plastic wrap, invert the top crust over the filling, and center on the filled crust. Peel off the top plastic wrap when the dough is centered. Trim the top crust to the same overhang as the bottom crust. Press the two crusts together and crimp the outer edges together. Freeze the whole pie for 15 minutes. Brush the crust with milk and sprinkle with the remaining ½ teaspoon of sugar. Prick the top crust several times with a fork or sharp knife to allow steam to escape. Place the pan on a nonstick rimmed baking sheet to catch drips.

5. Bake for 15 minutes on the lower rack to brown the bottom crust. Move the pie (still on the baking sheet) to the middle rack and bake another 30 to 35 minutes or until the crust is nicely browned. Cover loosely with foil or a pie shield if the edges brown too much. Cool completely on a wire rack before cutting.

WANT A SHINIER TOP CRUST? Brush it with an egg-wash (whole egg whisked with 1 teaspoon of water until foamy) instead of milk just before baking.

MAKING A SINGLE-CRUST PIE To make a single-crust pie, follow the recipe through Step 3, freezing the remaining half of dough for another pie. Finish the crust overhang with a decorative edge such as a crimp. Freeze the pie shell for 15 minutes, then prebake the crust, or fill and bake according to your recipe's instructions.

Per serving (½ of recipe), nutrients are calculated for pie crust only, divided by 4 servings: 90 calories; 2g protein; 16g total fat; 1g fiber; 35g carbohydrates; 16mg cholesterol; 163mg sodium

Preparation time: 15 minutes (plus time to make and chill the dough)
Freezing time: 15 minutes
Baking time: 45 to 50 minutes

Fillings for Small Double-Crust Pies

Ⓥ

Cherries and blueberries make fabulous pies, so here are two delicious pie fillings that you will make again and again. Each recipe makes enough filling for a 5- to 6-inch pie with 4 slices. The instructions include how to make these fillings into a complete pie.

Cherry Pie

MAKES ENOUGH FILLING
FOR A 5- TO 6-INCH PIE;
4 SLICES

2½ tablespoons granulated sugar (or more or less, depending on tartness of cherries)

1 teaspoon quick-cooking tapioca

1/32 teaspoon (smidgen) salt

¾ cup sour red cherries, well drained

¼ teaspoon almond extract

1 recipe for Small Double-Crust Pie (pages 202–203), to complete the pie

1 teaspoon unsalted butter or buttery spread, cut into small pieces

1. In a medium bowl, whisk together the sugar, tapioca, and salt until well blended. Stir in the cherries and almond extract until well blended. Let stand for 10 minutes to let the tapioca soften.

2. To finish the pie, start with Step 2 in Small Double-Crust Pie on pages 202–203. Fill the crust with the cherry filling, dot with the butter pieces, add top crust, and bake as directed.

Per slice (filling and double crust): 350 calories; 2g protein; 17g total fat; 1g fiber; 48g carbohydrates; 19mg cholesterol; 200mg sodium

Blueberry Pie

MAKES ENOUGH FILLING
FOR A 5- TO 6-INCH PIE;
4 SLICES

2 tablespoons granulated
sugar

2 teaspoons cornstarch

⅛ teaspoon (dash)
ground cinnamon

¹⁄₃₂ teaspoon (smidgen)
salt

¾ cup fresh blueberries

1 recipe Small Double-
Crust Pie (pages
202–203), to complete
the pie

1 teaspoon unsalted
butter or buttery spread,
cut into small pieces

Milk of choice, for
brushing

1. In a medium bowl, whisk together the sugar,
    cornstarch, cinnamon, and salt until blended. Gently
    stir in the blueberries until they are completely coated.
    Let stand for 5 minutes.

2. To finish the pie, start with Step 2 in Small Double-
    Crust Pie on pages 202–203. Fill the crust with the
    blueberry filling, dot with the butter pieces, add top
    crust, and bake as directed.

Per slice (filling and double crust): 345 calories; 2g protein;
17g total fat; 1g fiber; 47g carbohydrates; 19mg cholesterol;
198mg sodium

Rustic Peach Pie

Sometimes called a galette, *this free-form pie is one of the simplest to make and is virtually fail-proof because it works whether the pie is a perfect circle or not. That's why it is called rustic.*

MAKES 4 SLICES
(ONE 7-INCH PIE)

½ recipe Small Double-Crust Pie (pages 202–203)

1 fresh medium peach, peeled (if desired), pitted, and cut into 8 wedges

2 tablespoons granulated sugar (or to taste), plus 1 tablespoon for sprinkling

2 teaspoons cornstarch

1/16 teaspoon (pinch) salt

½ teaspoon pure almond extract

1 tablespoon milk of choice (or beaten egg), for wash

1 tablespoon apple jelly, for glazing (optional)

1. Make the Pie Crust recipe on pages 202–203, divide the dough in half, and freeze half for another recipe. Chill the remaining half, tightly wrapped, for 1 hour as directed.

2. Place racks in the bottom and middle positions of the oven. Preheat the oven to 375°F.

3. Cut a piece of parchment paper to fit a 9x13-inch rimmed baking sheet. Place the parchment on the countertop. Place the dough on the parchment and place a sheet of plastic wrap on top of the dough to prevent the rolling pin from sticking to the dough. Using a rolling pin, roll the dough to an 8-inch circle. To roll, move the rolling pin from the center of the dough to the outer edge, moving around the circle in clockwise fashion to assure uniform thickness. Transfer the pie dough (on the parchment) to the baking sheet; remove the plastic wrap. Push the edges of the crust toward the center to create a 7-inch circle with a rim that is about ¾ inch high; decoratively flute the rim. This is a rustic pie, so your circle does not have to be perfect—but it is important to create a higher rim around the edges to hold in the peach juices.

continued~

4. Gently toss the peach wedges in 2 tablespoons of the sugar, the cornstarch, salt, and almond extract. Arrange the wedges in a spiral in the pie crust. Sprinkle the peaches with the remaining 1 tablespoon sugar. Gently brush the milk on the outer crust rim to encourage browning.

5. Bake the pie on the bottom rack for 10 minutes, then transfer to the middle rack to bake for another 20 to 25 minutes, until the pie crust is nicely browned. Remove from the oven and gently brush the melted apple jelly on the peaches to add a little shine. Let the pie cool on the baking sheet to room temperature. Cut in half to serve.

Per slice: 330 calories; 2g protein; 1g total fat; 2g fiber; 73g carbohydrates; 1mg cholesterol; 42mg sodium

Apple Crisp

(V)

This homey dessert can bake while you eat dinner, enticing you with its cinnamon aroma. If your apples are not tart, reduce the sugar in the topping and filling by 1 teaspoon each. Cinnamon ice cream is nice with apples; to make, stir a little ground cinnamon into your favorite vanilla ice cream.

MAKES 2 SERVINGS

Topping

2 tablespoons Carol's Gluten-Free Flour Blend (page 24)

2 tablespoons gluten-free rolled oats*

1 tablespoon finely chopped walnuts (or your favorite nuts)

1 tablespoon unsalted butter or buttery spread, melted

2 teaspoons packed brown sugar

1/32 teaspoon (smidgen) salt

Filling

1 large Jonathan or Granny Smith apple, peeled, cored, and finely diced

1 tablespoon packed brown sugar

1 tablespoon melted unsalted butter or buttery spread, or canola oil

1 tablespoon lemon juice

1 teaspoon cornstarch

1/4 teaspoon ground cinnamon, apple pie spice, or pumpkin pie spice

1/32 teaspoon (smidgen) salt

1. Place a rack in the middle of the oven. Preheat the oven to 375°F. Grease two 3½x1¾-inch (4-ounce) ramekins.

2. Make the topping: In a medium bowl, mash together all the ingredients with a fork until crumbly. Alternatively, whirl in a mini-food processor until crumbly.

3. Make the filling: In a medium bowl, toss all the ingredients together until the apples are evenly coated. Divide the mixture and press firmly into the ramekins. Sprinkle the topping evenly on the apple mixture. Place the ramekins on a small rimmed baking sheet.

4. Bake the crisps until bubbly around the edges and lightly browned, about 30 minutes. Cool 10 minutes before serving.

Check with your physician to make sure oats are right for your diet.

Per serving: 340 calories; 3g protein; 15g total fat; 6g fiber; 53g carbohydrates; 31mg cholesterol; 107mg sodium

Raspberry Tartlets in Buttery Crust

Ⓥ

These cute little tarts are so simple, yet so gorgeous. The best part is that you just press the dough into the pans—no rolling pin needed! The fluted edge of the pan automatically shapes the dough. You will only use half of the dough, so freeze the other half for a later pair of tarts. I like the tartlets with a dollop of whipped cream or plain yogurt, but they are delicious by themselves.

MAKES 2 TARTLETS

Buttery Crust
½ cup Carol's Gluten-Free Flour Blend (page 24)

⅓ cup tapioca flour

¼ cup sweet rice flour

1 tablespoon granulated sugar

¼ teaspoon salt (or ¹⁄₁₆ teaspoon/ pinch if using buttery spread)

⅛ teaspoon (dash) xanthan gum

¹⁄₁₆ teaspoon (pinch) baking soda

6 tablespoons unsalted butter or buttery spread

3 tablespoons milk of choice

1 to 2 teaspoons water, if needed

Raspberry Filling
1 cup fresh raspberries

2 tablespoons good-quality raspberry jam (I like Bonne Maman, found in grocery stores)

1. Place racks in the bottom and middle positions of the oven. Preheat the oven to 375°F.

2. Make the crust: In a medium bowl, whisk together the flour blend, tapioca flour, sweet rice flour, sugar, salt, xanthan gum, and baking soda until well blended. With an electric mixer on low speed, beat in the butter and milk until small clumps form. If the dough shapes into a cohesive ball with your hands, it is ready. If not, beat in water, 1 teaspoon at a time, until the dough is ready. Knead the dough with your hands until it is very smooth.

3. Divide the dough in half. Tightly wrap one half and freeze for another use, for up to 1 month.

4. Divide the remaining dough in half and shape each half into a ball. Place one ball in the center of a 3½- to 4-inch nonstick tart pan. With your fingers, press the dough evenly on the bottom and up the sides of the pan. Repeat with the remaining dough half in a second tart pan. Place both pans on a rimmed baking sheet. With a fork, prick the bottoms and sides of the dough a few times.

5. Bake the crusts on the bottom rack of the oven for 5 minutes. Shift the pans to the higher rack and bake for another 10 minutes, until the edges of the pastry start to brown. Cool for 15 minutes on a wire rack.

6. Make the filling: Arrange the raspberries in a single layer in the two crusts. Heat the jam in the microwave on Low power just until the jam is melted, about 5 seconds. Pour the jam over the raspberries in each crust and use a pastry brush or fork to nudge the jam into the nooks and crannies between the raspberries and out to the edges of the crust. Let cool for at least 1 hour before serving.

Per tartlet: 385 calories; 2g protein; 18g total fat; 5g fiber; 55g carbohydrates; 47mg cholesterol; 192mg sodium

Preparation time: 10 minutes
Baking time: 30 to 35 minutes
Cooling/chilling time: 3 hours

New York–Style Cheesecake

Ⓥ

This is the basic, classic cheesecake, but in a miniature size with four perfectly proportioned servings. Try it topped with cherry pie filling or fresh berries or drained mandarin oranges. You can find 5-inch springform pans in kitchen stores or online. For best results, plan ahead to allow sufficient time for cooling and chilling.

MAKES 4 SLICES
(ONE 5-INCH CHEESECAKE)

⅓ cup gluten-free graham cracker crumbs, or vanilla or lemon-flavored cookie crumbs

2 teaspoons unsalted butter or buttery spread, melted

½ pound reduced-fat cream cheese or cream cheese alternative, at room temperature

1 tablespoon sour cream or sour cream alternative, at room temperature

¼ cup granulated sugar

1 teaspoon cornstarch

¹⁄₃₂ teaspoon (smidgen) salt

¼ teaspoon pure vanilla extract

1 large egg, at room temperature

1. Place a rack in the middle of the oven. Preheat the oven to 325°F. Generously grease the bottom and sides of a 5-inch nonstick springform pan (gray, not black).

2. In a small bowl, combine the crumbs and butter until well blended. With your fingers, press the mixture firmly onto the bottom of the pan. Bake just until the crust is fragrant, 5 to 7 minutes. Watch carefully, it burns quickly. Cool the crust while preparing the filling, but leave the oven on.

3. In a small bowl, with an electric mixer on medium speed, beat the cream cheese and sour cream until light and fluffy. Add the sugar, cornstarch, and salt and beat for 30 seconds, scraping the side of the bowl with a spatula. Beat in the vanilla and egg for 30 seconds. Use a spatula to spread the filling evenly over the crust.

4. Bake until the cheesecake looks firm on top and jiggles only slightly in the center, 30 to 35 minutes. It doesn't have to appear totally cooked. Turn the oven off, prop the oven door open with a wooden spoon, and let the cheesecake cool for 1 hour.

5. Refrigerate the cheesecake in the pan for at least 2 hours. Run a knife around the rim of the pan to loosen the edges, then remove the outer ring. Slide a thin metal spatula between the cheesecake and the bottom of the pan and gently slide the cheesecake onto a serving plate. To serve, use a sharp knife to cut into 4 slices, dipping the knife in hot water and then drying between each cut.

WATER BATH FOR A LIGHTER TEXTURE This recipe makes a dense cheesecake. For a lighter-textured version, bake it in a water bath: Place the springform pan in the middle of a 12-inch-square piece of aluminum foil and tightly wrap the bottom and side. Repeat with two more squares of foil so that the pan is encased in three layers of foil. Crimp the foil so that it is level with the top of the pan, and make sure the foil layers are pressed tightly all around to prevent water seepage. When the cheesecake is ready to bake, place the pan in an 8- or 9-inch metal pan (glass pans may shatter) and carefully pour boiling water into the metal pan to reach halfway up the sides of the springform pan, being careful not to splash onto the cheesecake. Bake as directed in Step 4.

Per slice: 300 calories; 9g protein; 15g total fat; 1g fiber; 33g carbohydrates; 84mg cholesterol; 568mg sodium

Chocolate Pudding Cakes (Mississippi Mud) ⓥ

There are many variations of this dish; we called it Chocolate Pudding Cake when I was growing up, but it is also known as Mississippi Mud. It is a combination of cake and pudding: gooey and decadent, yet miraculously egg-free. I bake it in individual ramekins but you can also bake it in a 5-inch cake pan. Garnish with whipped topping, or maybe ice cream or a dollop of marshmallow cream. Any way you eat it, it is a glorious, delicious muddle of honest-to-goodness comfort food!

MAKES 2 PUDDING CAKES

¼ cup Carol's Gluten-Free Flour Blend (page 24)

4 tablespoons granulated sugar, divided

4 teaspoons unsweetened Dutch-processed cocoa powder, sifted if clumpy, divided

¼ teaspoon baking powder

1⁄32 teaspoon (smidgen) salt

2 tablespoons milk of choice

2 teaspoons unsalted butter or buttery spread, melted and cooled slightly

¼ teaspoon pure vanilla extract

2 teaspoons packed brown sugar

4 tablespoons boiling water

2 tablespoons whipped topping (to make your own, see page 224), for garnish

Fresh berries, for garnish, such as raspberries, strawberries, or blueberries

1. Place a rack in the middle of the oven. Preheat the oven to 350°F. Generously grease two 3½x1¾-inch (4-ounce) ramekins.

2. In a small bowl, whisk together the flour blend, 3 tablespoons of the granulated sugar, 2 teaspoons of the cocoa powder, the baking powder, and salt until well blended. Whisk in the milk, butter, and vanilla until completely smooth. Divide evenly between the ramekins.

3. In a separate small bowl, whisk together the remaining 1 tablespoon granulated sugar, remaining 2 teaspoons cocoa powder, and the brown sugar until well blended. Sprinkle evenly over the batter. Very gently, pour 2 tablespoons of the boiling water over the topping in each ramekin.

4. Bake until the cakes are firm around the edges and the centers are slightly set, about 15 minutes. Cool for 10 minutes, then serve slightly warm with a dollop of whipped topping and fresh berries for garnish.

Per serving: 250 calories; 2g protein; 6g total fat; 2g fiber; 48g carbohydrates; 11mg cholesterol; 108mg sodium

Lemon Pudding Cakes ⓥ

This lemony dessert is called "pudding cake" because during baking an airy light cake rises to the top while the pudding sinks to the bottom. It is especially nice for beginners because it is delicious no matter how it turns out. I prefer to eat it warm while the pudding is still creamy, but it is also good at room temperature.

MAKES 2 PUDDING CAKES

1 large egg, separated, at room temperature

4 tablespoons granulated sugar, divided

1 tablespoon unsalted butter or buttery spread, at room temperature

Grated zest and juice of 1 medium lemon

1½ tablespoons cornstarch

⅓ cup milk of choice (the richer the better), at room temperature

$\frac{1}{32}$ teaspoon (smidgen) salt

Boiling water, for the water bath

1 teaspoon powdered sugar, for garnish

1. Place a rack in the lowest position of the oven. Preheat the oven to 325°F. Generously grease two 3½x1¾-inch (4-ounce) ramekins. Have a 9-inch square metal pan ready. (Do not use a glass pan, which could shatter from the boiling water.)

2. In a medium bowl, with an electric mixer on medium-low speed, beat the egg white until foamy. Increase the speed to medium and beat until soft peaks form. Gradually beat in 2 tablespoons of the sugar. Increase the speed to medium-high and continue beating until stiff peaks form, about 5 minutes from start to finish.

3. In another medium bowl—using the same beaters—with an electric mixer on low speed, beat the butter, lemon zest, and remaining 2 tablespoons of sugar for 1 minute. Beat in the egg yolk for 30 seconds. Beat in the cornstarch just until blended. Then beat in the lemon juice, milk, and salt until smooth. Gently whisk in the egg white mixture until no streaks remain. Divide the batter between the two ramekins. Place the ramekins in the metal pan and carefully pour boiling water into the larger pan until it is halfway up the sides of the ramekins, being careful not to splash on the puddings.

continued~

4. Bake until the cake pulls away from the edges of the ramekins and the top starts to brown, about 30 to 35 minutes. With oven mitts (a silicone mitt works well) or tongs, carefully transfer the ramekins to a wire rack to cool for 15 minutes. Serve warm or at room temperature, dusted with powdered sugar.

SOFT VS. STIFF PEAKS For soft peaks, the peaks of the beaten egg white should curl over slightly when you remove the beaters; for stiff peaks, they should stand straight up.

Per serving: 145 calories; 5g protein; 8g total fat; 1g fiber; 14g carbohydrates; 111mg cholesterol; 84mg sodium

Chocolate Pudding

This is a family favorite that I often whip up right before dinner so it's slightly cooled by dessert time. I prefer it a little warm, while my husband likes his chilled, so I enjoy mine right after dinner and he has his later, as a snack. Either way, it's delicious.

MAKES 2 SERVINGS
(½ CUP EACH)

¼ cup packed brown sugar

2 tablespoons unsweetened cocoa (either natural or Dutch-processed)

1½ tablespoons cornstarch

⅛ teaspoon (dash) salt

1 cup milk of choice (see Note)

1 teaspoon unsalted butter or buttery spread

½ teaspoon pure vanilla extract

Garnishes of choice, such as whipped topping, vanilla yogurt, fresh berries, or fresh mint

1. In a heavy, 1-quart saucepan, whisk together the sugar, cocoa, cornstarch, and salt until well blended. Gradually whisk in the milk until well blended. Place over medium heat and cook, stirring constantly with a heat-proof spatula, until the mixture starts to boil. Cook for 30 seconds, stirring constantly as it thickens. Remove from the heat.

2. Stir in the butter and vanilla until thoroughly blended. Pour into bowls and press a sheet of plastic wrap on the top to prevent a skin from forming. Let stand for 15 minutes and serve warm. Or refrigerate until firm, about 1 hour, and serve chilled.

NONDAIRY MILKS AND CORNSTARCH If using a low-protein nondairy milk (e.g., coconut, flax, hemp, or rice), increase cornstarch to 2 tablespoons.

Per serving: 210 calories; 5g protein; 4g total fat; 2g fiber; 42g carbohydrates; 10mg cholesterol; 229mg sodium

Chocolate Mousse

(V)

This decadent mousse carries some secret nutritional boosts. Tofu adds protein, and avocado lends creamy smoothness and healthy fats—all without you knowing they're there. This dessert is perfect for a romantic dinner for two, or for an everyday treat that is healthier than most mousses. I like to vary the liqueurs, but we usually opt for coffee liqueur because it goes so well with chocolate.

MAKES 2 SERVINGS
(A GENEROUS ½ CUP
EACH)

½ medium ripe avocado, pitted and cubed

¾ cup soft silken tofu, drained

½ cup milk of choice

3 tablespoons gluten-free chocolate syrup

2 tablespoons unsweetened cocoa (either natural or Dutch-process)

1 tablespoon coffee or chocolate liqueur or milk of choice

½ teaspoon pure vanilla extract

¹⁄₁₆ teaspoon (pinch) salt

Garnishes of choice, such as whipped topping, vanilla yogurt, fresh berries, or mint

1. Place all ingredients in a blender (I use a mini-blender called a Magic Bullet) and whirl until thoroughly blended, scraping down the sides at least once.

2. Divide between two dessert bowls or wine goblets. Cover with plastic wrap and chill for at least 1 hour. Serve plain or garnished, as you wish.

LEFTOVER AVOCADO AND TOFU Slice the leftover avocado onto a salad or use it in a Mexican dish. Store the leftover tofu, covered, in the refrigerator for up to 1 week and make another Chocolate Mousse. Or, add it to your morning smoothie for extra protein.

Per serving: 275 calories; 8g protein; 11g total fat; 2g fiber; 32g carbohydrates; 2mg cholesterol; 145mg sodium

Vanilla Pudding ⓥ

This is a dessert staple because you can jazz it up in many different ways. Add sliced bananas and gluten-free vanilla cookies for a Southern-style banana pudding. A half-teaspoon grated lemon zest transforms it into a lemon pudding. Or, instead of vanilla extract, use ¼ teaspoon peppermint or almond extract. For a cream pie, pour the pudding into a pre-baked 5-inch pie crust (see Small Double-Crust Pie on pages 202–203). The possibilities are endless.

MAKES 2 SERVINGS
(½ CUP EACH)

¾ cup whole milk or other milk of choice

2 large egg yolks

3 tablespoons granulated sugar

1 tablespoon cornstarch

¹⁄₁₆ teaspoon (pinch) salt (or ¹⁄₃₂ teaspoon/smidgen if using buttery spread)

1½ teaspoons unsalted butter or buttery spread

½ teaspoon pure vanilla extract

Garnishes of choice, such as fresh fruit, fresh mint, or chopped walnuts

1. Measure the milk in a 2-cup measuring cup. Whisk the egg yolks into the milk until thoroughly blended.

2. In a heavy 2-quart saucepan, whisk together the sugar, cornstarch, and salt until well blended. Slowly whisk in the egg mixture until very smooth. Place the saucepan over medium heat and cook, whisking constantly, until the pudding thickens, 5 to 7 minutes (depending on the type of milk used). Remove from the heat.

3. Stir in the butter and vanilla until smooth. Pour into a bowl and press a sheet of plastic wrap on top to prevent a skin from forming. Chill for 2 hours. Spoon into dessert goblets, small wine glasses, or small martini glasses. Garnish as desired and serve.

LEFTOVER EGG WHITES Use the leftover egg whites in Coconut Macaroons (page 177) or scrambled eggs.

Per serving: 230 calories; 6g protein; 11g total fat; 1g fiber; 27g carbohydrates; 233mg cholesterol; 53mg sodium

Tapioca Pudding

When I was a little girl, my mother made tapioca pudding for me whenever I was sick. I guess it was such a comforting dish that she thought it would make me feel better. Today, whenever I make it, I think of my mother—but I prefer it as a dessert instead of a curative. She used whole cow's milk, but I have successfully made it with 2% milk, hemp milk, rice milk, soy milk, and canned coconut milk. Each type of milk lends its own subtlety; my nondairy favorites are hemp milk and coconut milk.

MAKES 2 SERVINGS
(½ CUP EACH)

1 cup milk of choice

1 large egg

2 tablespoons granulated sugar

1 tablespoon minute tapioca

½ teaspoon pure vanilla extract

1. In a heavy 2-quart saucepan, whisk together the milk, egg, sugar, and tapioca until well blended. Let stand for 5 minutes.

2. Place the pan over medium heat and cook, whisking constantly, until the pudding comes to a full boil. Remove from the heat and stir in the vanilla. Let stand for 20 minutes.

3. Spoon into dessert bowls, goblets, or small wine glasses and serve immediately; or, for a cold pudding, chill for at least 2 hours.

Fancier Tapioca Pudding: This is delicious served plain, but for variety add a dollop of whipped cream, cherry pie filling, or fresh fruit (such as berries, mandarin oranges, halved green grapes, or sliced kiwi) to dress it up a bit.

Per serving: 160 calories; 7g protein; 3g total fat; 1g fiber; 26g carbohydrates; 96mg cholesterol; 125mg sodium

Cinnamon-Raisin Bread Pudding with Rum Sauce

Ⓥ

Here's the perfect use for leftover gluten-free cinnamon-raisin bread. If using plain bread, increase the raisins to 3 tablespoons. This recipe uses a store-bought loaf (Udi's Gluten Free) that has small slices.

MAKES 2 SERVINGS

Bread Pudding

1½ cups ½-inch cubed gluten-free cinnamon-raisin bread (about 2 slices)

2 tablespoons dark raisins

⅔ cup milk of choice (the richer the better)

¼ cup packed brown sugar

1 large egg, at room temperature

½ teaspoon pure vanilla extract

⅛ teaspoon (dash) ground cinnamon

1/16 teaspoon (pinch) ground nutmeg (optional)

1/16 teaspoon (pinch) salt

Rum Sauce

1 tablespoon granulated sugar

½ teaspoon cornstarch

⅛ teaspoon (dash) ground cinnamon

1/32 teaspoon (smidgen) salt

2 tablespoons water

1 tablespoon rum, or 1 teaspoon rum extract (optional)

¼ teaspoon unsalted butter or buttery spread

1. Place a rack in the middle of the oven. Preheat the oven to 325°F. Generously grease two 3½x2-inch (6-ounce) ramekins and place on a small baking sheet.

2. Make the bread pudding: Divide the cubed bread between the ramekins and sprinkle the raisins on top. Whisk together the milk, brown sugar, egg, vanilla, cinnamon, nutmeg, and salt until smooth. Pour evenly over the bread cubes and press down on the bread to submerge each bread cube in the liquid. Let stand 15 minutes.

3. Cover each ramekin with aluminum foil. Bake 15 minutes. Remove the foil and press the bread cubes down with a spatula. Bake another 15 to 20 minutes, until the tops are browned. Cool the bread pudding on a wire rack for 10 minutes.

4. Meanwhile, make the rum sauce: In a small saucepan over medium heat, whisk together granulated sugar, cornstarch, cinnamon, and salt. Whisk in the water and rum and bring to a boil, whisking constantly. Cook until the sauce thickens slightly, about 2 minutes. Remove from the heat and stir in the butter until melted.

5. Serve the bread pudding warm, topped with a tablespoon of the rum sauce.

Per serving: 350 calories; 9g protein; 4g total fat; 2g fiber; 66g carbohydrates; 98mg cholesterol; 281mg sodium

Preparation time: 10 minutes
Baking time: 90 minutes
Cooling time: 1½ hours

Pavlova with Raspberries ⓥ

The exact history of this light, airy dessert of meringue, whipped cream, and fruit is vague, but it is usually associated with Australia because an Australian chef supposedly made it for the visiting Russian ballerina Anna Pavlova. Regardless of its provenance, it's delightful and naturally gluten free. I use fresh raspberries and raspberry jam here, but any colorful fruit and jam combination will work.

MAKES 2 PAVLOVAS

1 large egg white, at room temperature

⅟₃₂ teaspoon (smidgen) salt

2 tablespoons granulated sugar

1 teaspoon cornstarch

⅟₁₆ teaspoon (pinch) distilled vinegar

⅟₃₂ teaspoon (smidgen) pure vanilla extract

½ cup whipped topping (to make your own, see page 224)

¼ cup fresh raspberries, or to taste

2 tablespoons raspberry jam, or to taste

1 teaspoon water, if needed

1. Place a rack in the middle of the oven. Preheat the oven to 250°F. Line a 9x13-inch baking sheet (not nonstick) with parchment paper. With a pencil, outline two 4-inch circles in the center of the parchment paper; flip the paper over (to avoid getting pencil lead on the meringue).

2. In a medium bowl, with an electric mixer on medium speed, beat the egg white and salt until firm. Gradually beat in the sugar, 1 tablespoon at a time, until the meringue stands in soft peaks. With a rubber spatula, gently fold in the cornstarch until blended, then fold in the vinegar and vanilla.

3. Spread the meringues on the two marked circles. Using a spoon or spatula, make a large indentation in the center of each meringue to hold the filling.

4. Bake the meringues for 90 minutes, until the centers are firm and the edges are set. Turn off the oven, keep the door closed, and let the meringues cool for 1 hour. Transfer to a wire rack to cool completely.

continued~

5. To assemble, use a thin spatula to remove the meringues carefully from the parchment and place on two serving plates. Take care; the meringues shatter easily. Fill each indentation with ¼ cup whipped topping. Top with the raspberries. Stir a teaspoon of water into the jam to thin it a bit if needed. Drizzle the jam over the raspberries, letting some drizzle down the sides of the meringue. Serve immediately.

Homemade Whipped Topping To make your own whipped topping, in a small bowl with an electric mixer on medium speed, beat 2 tablespoons heavy cream until soft peaks form. Beat in 1 teaspoon granulated sugar and ¼ teaspoon pure vanilla extract. Serve immediately. Makes ½ cup whipped topping.

Per pavlova: 150 calories; 2g protein; 2g total fat; 1g fiber; 31g carbohydrates; 0mg cholesterol; 71mg sodium

Tiramisu

Ⓥ

I love this Italian dessert for its decadence and creamy smoothness—not to mention that it is also no-cook and super easy. Traditional versions use shallow bowls (hard to serve from) and ladyfingers (hard to find in gluten-free form). To make things easier, I assemble the dessert in two small ramekins and use store-bought gluten-free cookies as the base. I like Pamela's gluten-free cookies—especially the dark chocolate chunk and pecan shortbread varieties. The usual mascarpone is replaced with regular cream cheese and sour cream so you don't have leftover mascarpone.

MAKES 2 SERVINGS

½ cup (4 ounces) reduced-fat cream cheese or cream cheese alternative, at room temperature

¼ cup light sour cream or sour cream alternative, at room temperature

3 tablespoons granulated sugar

2 tablespoons milk of choice, or water

½ teaspoon pure vanilla extract

2 tablespoons brewed espresso, or 1 teaspoon instant espresso powder dissolved in 2 tablespoons hot water

1 tablespoon coffee liqueur, rum, or brandy (or more espresso)

2 (2-inch) gluten-free cookies

2 teaspoons unsweetened cocoa powder (either Dutch-processed or natural), for dusting

2 teaspoons grated bittersweet or semi-sweet chocolate, for garnish

1. Coat two 3½x1¾-inch (4-ounce) ramekins with cooking spray or lightly grease with canola oil.

2. In a small bowl, with a spatula, beat together the cream cheese, sour cream, sugar, milk, and vanilla until smooth. Spread ¼ cup evenly in each ramekin.

3. In a small, shallow bowl, combine the espresso and liqueur. Holding a cookie parallel to the espresso mixture, quickly and lightly dip in the espresso mixture only halfway and place it in a ramekin; repeat with the remaining cookie and ramekin. (If there is any espresso mixture left, drizzle it into the ramekins.) Evenly divide the remaining cream cheese mixture and spread evenly on top of each cookie with a spatula. Tap each ramekin on the countertop to settle the contents evenly. Place the cocoa in a fine-mesh sieve and gently dust on top of each ramekin.

4. Cover each ramekin with plastic wrap and refrigerate for at least 4 hours or up to 24 hours. Serve, garnished with grated chocolate.

Per serving: 400 calories; 9g protein; 21g total fat; 2g fiber; 45g carbohydrates; 35mg cholesterol; 47mg sodium

Cream Cheese Frosting (V)

This recipe makes a generous amount of frosting for four cupcakes, perfect for the small household. This is the traditional frosting for Red Velvet Cupcakes (page 195) and Carrot Cake Cupcakes (page 196). If there are any leftovers (fat chance!) refrigerate them because of the cream cheese, which can go bad at room temperature. The corn syrup adds a lovely sheen, but is optional.

MAKES ½ CUP
(8 TABLESPOONS)

2 tablespoons reduced-fat cream cheese or cream cheese alternative, at room temperature

½ teaspoon pure vanilla extract

¼ teaspoon corn syrup (optional)

1 cup powdered sugar

½ teaspoon water, or more, as needed

In a small bowl, with an electric mixer on low speed, beat the cream cheese, vanilla, and corn syrup (if using) until completely smooth. (Alternatively, you can mix by hand with a spatula.) Gradually beat in the powdered sugar until completely blended. If the frosting is too stiff to spread, beat in the ½ teaspoon water until smooth. If the frosting is still too stiff, beat in ¼ teaspoon more water and continue beating until the frosting is spreadable. If you accidentally add too much water, add more powdered sugar, 1 tablespoon at a time, until you reach the desired consistency. Use immediately and refrigerate any leftovers.

Per tablespoon: 70 calories; 1g protein; 1g total fat; 0g fiber; 15g carbohydrates; 2mg cholesterol; 25mg sodium

Vanilla–Powdered Sugar Frosting

This is the classic vanilla frosting, perfect for anything you like—cakes, cupcakes, muffins. If you want a drizzling consistency, add water, 1 teaspoon at a time, to reach the stage you want. This recipe makes enough frosting to generously frost 4 cupcakes or 2 mini-cakes. The corn syrup adds a lovely sheen, but is optional.

MAKES ¾ CUP
(12 TABLESPOONS)

1 cup powdered sugar

¹⁄₃₂ teaspoon (smidgen) salt

1 tablespoon canola oil, or slightly cooled melted unsalted butter or buttery spread

1 tablespoon water, or more as needed

¼ teaspoon pure vanilla extract

¼ teaspoon corn syrup (optional)

In a small bowl, whisk together the powdered sugar and salt. With an electric mixer on low speed, beat in the oil, water, vanilla, and corn syrup (if using) until the frosting is smooth and spreadable. If the frosting is too stiff to spread, beat in more water, 1 teaspoon at a time, until the frosting is spreadable. Use immediately.

Per tablespoon: 50 calories; 0g protein; 1g total fat; 0g fiber; 10g carbohydrates; 0mg cholesterol; 11mg sodium

Chocolate–Powdered Sugar Frosting

Ⓥ

Use this anywhere you want a chocolate frosting. I like it on the Flourless Chocolate Cake (page 191), but it is also delightful on anything that is complemented by chocolate. The recipe makes enough frosting for 6 cupcakes or 2 mini-cakes. The corn syrup ensures a shinier frosting that stays soft longer, but it is optional.

MAKES ¾ CUP
(12 TABLESPOONS)

1 cup powdered sugar

1 tablespoon unsweetened cocoa powder

$\frac{1}{32}$ teaspoon (smidgen) salt

1 tablespoon canola oil, or slightly cooled melted unsalted butter or buttery spread

4 teaspoons water

¼ teaspoon pure vanilla extract

¼ teaspoon corn syrup (optional)

In a small bowl, whisk together the powdered sugar, cocoa, and salt. With an electric mixer on low speed, beat in the oil, water, vanilla, and corn syrup (if using) until the frosting is smooth and spreadable. If the frosting is too stiff to spread, beat in more water, 1 teaspoon at a time, until the frosting is spreadable. Use immediately.

Per tablespoon: 50 calories; 1g protein; 1g total fat; 1g fiber; 10g carbohydrates; 0mg cholesterol; 6mg sodium

Fluffy White Cooked Frosting

Ⓥ

Egg white is the secret behind this fluffy frosting. When whipped over simmering water, it transforms into the most gorgeous white frosting you can imagine. The recipe makes enough for 6 cupcakes or 2 mini-cakes; it must be used right after it's made because it starts to set up and harden.

MAKES ABOUT 1 CUP
(16 TABLESPOONS)

1 large egg white, at room temperature

6 tablespoons granulated sugar

1/16 teaspoon (pinch) cream of tartar

1 tablespoon cold water

1/4 teaspoon pure vanilla extract

1. In a double boiler over simmering water (don't let the bottom of the double boiler touch the water), with a handheld electric mixer on medium speed, beat the egg white, sugar, cream of tartar, and water until the frosting becomes very white and fluffy and soft peaks form, 3 to 4 minutes.

2. Remove the double boiler from the heat and stir in the vanilla. Use the frosting immediately before it starts to set.

Per tablespoon: 20 calories; 1g protein; 0g total fat; 0g fiber; 5g carbohydrates; 0mg cholesterol; 4mg sodium

Sources

National Associations

Several non-profit associations provide a wealth of information on the gluten-free lifestyle, including newsletters, magazines, and Web sites. Many hold conferences and also sponsor support groups in many cities, so check to see if one is in your area.

- Celiac Disease Foundation (www.celiac.org)
- Celiac Sprue Association (www.csaceliacs.org)
- Gluten Intolerance Group (www.gluten.net)
- Beyond Celiac, formerly known as National Foundation for Celiac Awareness (www.beyondceliac.org)

Magazines

These are lovely, full-color magazines available by subscription. Some can be found on magazine stands.

- *Easy Eats* (www.easyeats.com)
- *Delight Gluten-Free* (www.delightglutenfree.com)
- *Gluten-Free Living* (www.glutenfreeliving.com)
- *Gluten-Free and More,* formerly *Living Without* (www.glutenfreeandmore.com)
- *Simply Gluten-Free* (www.simplygluten-free.com)

Universities and Medical Centers

Many universities and medical centers have established research centers that conduct research, diagnose patients, hold conferences, and offer a wealth of information on their Web sites.

- Celiac Center at Harvard University-Beth Israel
  www.bidmc.org
- Celiac Center at Paoli Hospital
  http://www.mainlinehealth.org/paoliceliac

- Celiac Disease Center, Columbia University
  http://celiaccenter.ucsd.org
- Celiac Disease Clinic, Mayo Clinic
  www.mayoclinic.org
- Center for Celiac Research, Massachusetts General Hospital
  (formerly at the University of Maryland)
  www.celiaccenter.org
- Colorado Center for Celiac Disease at Children's Hospital
  www.childrenscolorado.org/celiac
- Jefferson Celiac Center
  http://www.jeffersonhospital.org/departments-and-services/celiac-center
- University of Chicago Celiac Disease Center
  www.cureceliacdisease.org
- William K. Warren Medical Research Center for Celiac Disease,
  University of California at San Diego
  http://health.ucsd.edu/specialties/gastro/areas-expertise/Pages/celiac-disease
  -clinic.aspx

An excellent book that will help you understand the nutritional aspects of the gluten-free diet is *Gluten-Free: The Definitive Resource Guide,* by Shelley Case, RD (Case Nutrition Consulting, 2016). Also visit www.shelleycase.com.

Acknowledgments

Like many books, this one had its roots in a simple observation of how America lives: I noticed that many people, like me, live in small households and the typical recipe with 4 to 6 servings was simply too large for practical everyday living.

While there were many resources for small families in general, little was available for those of us with gluten-free lifestyles. So, I decided to fill that void — using my own empty-nester, two-person household (hubby and me) as the experimental kitchen to develop perfectly proportioned recipes for two.

First and foremost, thanks to my wonderful editor at Houghton Mifflin Harcourt, Cindy Kitchel and her assistant Melissa Fisch, for recognizing the need for this book and for their valuable insights. I SO appreciate you both! Photographer Tom Hirschfeld captured the beauty of these foods to entice you. I also want to thank the staff at Houghton Mifflin Harcourt, especially art director Melissa Lotfy, designer Alison Wilkes, copy editor Deri Reed, and production editor Helen Seachrist.

And special thanks to my marvelous agent of nearly two decades, Lisa Ekus, for her support, encouragement, and friendship all these years. Lisa saw the need for this book long ago, so thanks for standing by me all these years.

I have a fantastic group of recipe testers across the country who gave me extremely valuable feedback. They come from all walks of life, geographical locations, culinary backgrounds, and tastes, but they have one thing in common: They either live in or cook for a small household — usually two people. They baked, roasted, braised, microwaved, and fried in their own kitchens, and then told me how the food looked and how it tasted — often with input from their (thankfully) cooperative spouses, friends, acquaintances, and colleagues. They are Janet L. Armil, Rose Baluha, Anne Barfield, Susan Cox-Gilbertson, Carol Graham, Mary Guerriero (who was diagnosed in 1991 and is also intolerant to tapioca, amaranth, quinoa, and hemp), Cheryl Hutchinson, Kelli McCaffrey, Nancy Merrill, Janet Y. Rinehart of the Houston Celiac Support Group, Charlene Travelstead, and Cecile Hankey Weed. I truly appreciate all of you; this cookbook could not have been written without your help.

Now that you know why I wrote this book and recognize all the many people who made it possible, I hope you enjoy these recipes.

Index

Note: Page references in *italics* indicate photographs.